United States Congress, War Dept. of the United States,
Robert T. Lincoln, Elisha Baxter

Letter From the Secretary of War

Transmitting in Response to Senate Resolution of the 18th of January,

1883

United States Congress, War Dept. of the United States, Robert T. Lincoln, Elisha Baxter

Letter From the Secretary of War
Transmitting in Response to Senate Resolution of the 18th of January, 1883

ISBN/EAN: 9783337163068

Printed in Europe, USA, Canada, Australia, Japan

Cover: Foto ©Suzi / pixelio.de

More available books at **www.hansebooks.com**

LETTER

FROM

THE SECRETARY OF WAR.

TRANSMITTING,

In response to Senate resolution of the 18th of January, 1883, a report, dated the 2d instant, from Adjutant-General of the Army, and accompanying copies of papers, relating to the payment of the Fourth Arkansas Mounted Infantry Volunteers.

FEBRUARY 5, 1883.—Referred to the Committee on Military Affairs and ordered to be printed.

WAR DEPARTMENT,
Washington City, February 3, 1883.

The Secretary of War has the honor to transmit to the United States Senate a report, dated the 2d instant, from the Adjutant General of the Army, and its accompanying copies of papers, in response to Senate resolution of the 18th ultimo, as follows:

Resolved, That the Secretary of War be directed to inform the Senate what action has been taken under the provisions of the resolution approved March 18, 1870, "providing for the payment of the Fourth Arkansas Mounted Infantry Volunteers," and to furnish copies of all papers, correspondence, and muster rolls on file in his department relating to said organization.

ROBERT T. LINCOLN,
Secretary of War.

The PRESIDENT *pro tempore*
of the United States Senate.

WAR DEPARTMENT,
ADJUTANT-GENERAL'S OFFICE,
Washington, February 2, 1883.

SIR: I have the honor to return herewith a resolution of the United States Senate, dated the 18th ultimo, directing the Secretary of War to inform the Senate what action has been taken under the provisions of the joint resolution approved March 18, 1870, "providing for the payment of the Fourth Arkansas Mounted Infantry Volunteers"; also, to furnish copies of all papers, correspondence, and muster-rolls on file in the department relating to said organization, and to report as follows:

It has been found impracticable to carry out the provisions of said joint resolution, for the reasons set forth in report of August 17, 1882, from this office to the honorable Secretary of War, a copy of which is embraced in the copies of papers transmitted herewith in compliance with the resolution of the Senate.

It is proper to remark that nothing has occurred since said report was made to change or modify the views therein expressed.

I am, sir, very respectfully, your obedient servant,

R. C. DRUM,
Adjutant-General.

The Hon. the SECRETARY OF WAR.

COPIES OF PAPERS, CORRESPONDENCE, ETC., ON FILE IN THE WAR DE-PARTMENT RELATING TO THE FOURTH ARKANSAS MOUNTED INFANTRY VOLUNTEERS.

[Furnished in compliance with a resolution of the Senate, dated January 18, 1883.]

LITTLE ROCK, ARK., April 12th, A. D. 1864.

GENERAL: I have the honor to state that in November last I obtained authority from Maj. Gen. Steele to recruit a reg't of men to be mustered into the service of the U. S. for the term of twelve months, upon which authority I proceeded to enlist three hundred and sixty men, who are now in camps at Batesville, in the N. E. district of Arks., clothed, armed, and equipped, and provisioned by the U. S., most of whom have been performing the most active duties for three months past. These men are almost entirely Arkansians, and having thus openly committed themselves to the Union cause cannot go back to their homes. I therefore respectfully ask for explicit authority to have these men and a sufficient no. of others to complete a full regiment, mustered into the U. S. service for the term of twelve months, and if practicable as cavalry. In the event of a refusal to accept them as U. S. troops, I will be pleased to know whether the U. S. would not arm, equip, and pay them as State troops for the term of twelve months. It is highly advisable that you telegraph the answer, as I hope to accomplish something by way of having the legislature of Arkansas, now in session, to accept them as State troops in case of a refusal of the department to muster them as U. S. troops.

I have the honor, gen'l, to be your ob't serv't,

E. BAXTER.
Col. & Recruiting Officer.

The ADJUTANT-GENERAL OF THE WAR DEPARTMENT.

[Indorsement.]

HEADQUARTERS DEPT. OF ARKANSAS,
Little Rock, April 20th, 1864.

Respectfully forwarded to the War Department, with the recommendation that the authority asked for by Col. Baxter be granted.

F. STEELE,
Maj. Gen'l Com'd'g, in absence of the General.
By W. D. GREEN,
Ass't Adj't Gen'l.

[Telegram.]

HEADQUARTERS SUPERINTENDENT VOLUNTEER RECRUITING SERVICE,
CHIEF MUSTERING AND DISBURSING OFFICE,
Little Rock, Ark., April 20th, 1864.

Col. JAMES B. FRY,
Pro. Mar. Gen'l, Washington, D. C.:

There are three hundred and fifty men garrisoning the post at Batesville, enlisted by Colonel Baxter for twelve months, by authority from Gen'l Steele dated last October. They have been in active service since enlistment, without pay. The colonel assures me they will enlist for three years, if their muster can be dated back to time of original enlistment and they can now receive pay and benefits arising from a muster of such date. Can it be done?

J. W. SWAIN,
Capt. and Supt. Vol. Rec. Service.

[Special Orders No. 110.]

HEADQUARTERS DIST. SOUTHWEST MO.,
Springfield, Mo., April 24, 1864.

[Extract.]

* * * * * * *

2. Capt. John G. Quinn, asst. com's'y of musters, Dist. S. W. Mo., is authorized to muster the recruits brought from Yellville, Arkansas, by Commissary Sergeant James B. Ennis, 6th M. S. M. Cav., into the 4th Regt., Arkansas Inf'y. Vols., being organized by Col. Baxter, at Batesville, Arkansas.

He will furnish the men, when mustered into the service, with subsistence and clothing, and will draw arms and ammunition for their protection and use until they join their regiment for duty.

* * * * * * *

By order of Brigadier Sanborn.

W. D. HUBBARD,
1st Lieut. and Acting Asst. Adjt. General.

[Telegram.]

PROVOST MARSHAL GENERAL'S OFFICE,
April 27, 1864.

Capt. JAS. W. SWAIN, Supt. Vol. R. S., Little Rock, Arkansas:

The three hundred (300) men at Batesville may be enlisted for three (3) years, and musters dated back to cover twelve (12) months term.

In so doing no right or claim will be granted for any other bounty than the one hundred dollars provided by act of 1861.

J. B. FRY,
Pro. Mar. Gen'l.

[Special Orders No. 121.]

HEADQUARTERS DEPARTMENT OF ARKANSAS, &C.,
Little Rock, Ark., June 2d, 1864.

* * * * * * *

2. The authority heretofore granted for for the enlistment for one year of a regiment of Arkansas troops, to be designated the 4th Arkansas Mounted Infantry, not having been confirmed by the War Department, the organization is hereby disbanded.

All quartermasters' property and ordnance stores in the possession of the battalion will be turned over to the proper staff officers at Duvall's Bluff.

* * * * * * *

By order of Maj. General F. Steele.

BENJ. B. FOSTER,
Asst. Adjt. General.

The following letter was referred to the War Dept. by Hon. Henry Wilson, U. S. S.:

CENTRALIA, ILL., January 20th, 1865.

Hon. HENRY WILSON,
Chairman of the Senate Military Committee:

DEAR SIR: By virtue of an order from Maj. Genl. F. Steele, commanding the Dept. of Arks., of which the enclosed is a correct copy, I proceeded to recruit a regt. for the U. S. service designated as the 4th Arkansas Mounted Infantry, and commanded them in the field (doing the most active service) until, in consequence of my election to the U. S. Senate, I was relieved and Captain T. A. Baxter assigned to the command, under whom the men continued to do duty until some time in June last, when, by operation of an order from the War Dept., they were disbanded on the ground that they were twelve-months men.

In the mean time many of these men and officers were several times mustered for pay, but others, enlisting at a later date, &c., were not even mustered for pay, whilst none were mustered into the service.

Most of the men furnished their own horses, and many were killed and their horses lost in action with the enemy.

I learn that there is no law by which these men can be paid for their service and property, and I know of no one upon whom I can more appropriately call to insist upon Congress for such legislation as will enable the officers and men of this command to obtain such pay for service and loss of property as officers and men of the same rank regularly mustered into the volunteer service of the U. S., than yourself.

I need scarcely remind you that in legislating on this subject you should bear in mind that records in this case are very scant, and that the terms of your bill should cover all intent of muster-rolls and such other records as usually called for by the paymaster.

You will doubtless recollect me as one of the parties bearing credentials to the U. S. Senate from the State of Arkansas at your last session. Having been partially rejected (though I am at a loss to know on what grounds), I have not thought proper to visit Washington again. Hence this communication instead of a personal interview.

May I not hope, sir, that you will for a time devote your eminent influence and position to the interest of this unfortunate band of men, than whom there is not a more patriotic class of men in the world, and that I may hear from you soon and favorably, in regard to the legislation asked for.

With high regard, I have the honor to be,

E. BAXTER.

HEADQUARTERS ARMY OF ARKANSAS,
Little Rock, Oct. 23d, 1863.

Elisha Baxter, of Batesville, Independence County, State of Arkansas, is hereby authorized to raise a regiment of infantry to be mustered into the United States service for the term of one year, or during the war, if not sooner discharged.

The headquarters for the recruiting will be at Batesville, Independence County, and all persons recruiting for said regiment will be governed by the regulations for the recruiting service and orders from War Department, Department of Missouri, and these headquarters.

Mr. Baxter will report to these headquarters for such instructions as he may require.
By order of Maj. Gen'l F. Steele.

A. H. RYAN,
Capt. & A. D. C.

WAR DEPARTMENT, ADJUTANT-GENERAL'S OFFICE,
February 18, 1865.

Hon. HENRY WILSON,
   U. S. S., Washington, D. C.:

SIR: I have the honor to acknowledge the receipt of your reference of the letter of Mr. E. Baxter, late colonel 4 Arkansas Mounted Infantry, asking that the officers and men of that command may receive the same pay as though mustered into service, and that they be paid for loss of property.

In reply I am directed to inform you that there are no records of any organization known as the 4th Arkansas Mounted Infantry on file in this office, and therefore no action can be taken in this case.

I am, sir, very respectfully, your obedient servant,
THOMAS M. VINCENT,
Assistant Adjutant-General.

WASHINGTON, D. C.,
December 22nd, 1865.

ADJUTANT-GENERAL, ARMY OF THE UNITED STATES:

SIR: On the 23d of October, A. D. 1863, I received the following order, viz:

HEADQUARTERS ARMY OF ARKANSAS,
October 23d, A. D. 1863.

Elisha Baxter, of Batesville, Independence County, State of Arkansas, is hereby authorized to raise a regiment of infantry to be mustered into the service of the U. S. for the term of one year, or during the war, if not sooner discharged.

The headquarters for the recruiting will be at Batesville, Independence County, and all persons recruiting for said regiment will be governed by the regulations for the recruiting service and orders from the War Department, Department of Missouri, and these headquarters.

Mr. Baxter will report to these headquarters for such instructions as he may require.
By order of Maj. Gen'l F. Steele.

A. H. RYAN,
Capt. and A. D. C.

Under authority of this order, I proceeded to recruit and command in the field until the organization was nearly complete, when I was relieved by the following order:

[Special Order No. 91.]

HEADQUARTERS DEPART. OF ARKS.,
Little Rock, Arks., May the 3d, 1864.

VIII. Hon. E. Baxter, recruiting officer for the 4th Arkansas Mounted Infantry, having been elected to the Senate of the United States from the State of Arkansas, is hereby relieved from duty with the regiment, and will turn over his command and all orders and instructions he may have received relating to the organization of the same to Capt. T. A. Baxter, 4th Arkansas Mounted Infantry, subject to the approval of the War Dept.

By order of Maj. Gen'l F. Steele.

W. D. GREEN,
Assistant Adjutant-General.

In the mean time all the officers and men under my command performed active duty from the date of their respective enlistment until they were disbanded; quite a number of the men were killed and wounded in actions, and many of their horses were killed and captured by the enemy.

Finally, the organization was disbanded by the following order, without even being mustered:

[Special Order No. 121.]

[Extract.]

II. The authority heretofore granted for the enlistment for one year of a regiment of Arkansas troops, to be designated the 4th Arkansas Mounted Infantry, not having been confirmed by the War Department, the organization is hereby disbanded.

All quartermaster's property and ordnance stores in the possession of the batallion will be turned over to the proper staff officers at Devall's Bluff.

By order of Major-General F. Steele.

W. D. GREEN,
Assistant Adjutant-General.

From the foregoing you will see that the regiment has been raised for the service of the United States; that they actually performed service, and underwent all the privations and hardships incident to a soldier's life. Yet as I understand the case, they cannot put up any legal claim to pay for service so rendered. The object of this communication therefore is to procure from your department such information and suggestions as will enable me to procure such legislation as will allow the officers and men of my command pay for the service so rendered.

I am, gen'l, very respectfully,

E. BAXTER,
Senator elect from Arkansas.

WAR DEPARTMENT, ADJUTANT-GENERAL'S OFFICE,
Washington, January 2, 1866.

Hon. E. BAXTER,
Washington, D. C.:

SIR: I have the honor to acknowledge the receipt of your letter of the 22nd ultimo requesting information concerning the force recruited under the authority granted October 23, 1863, by Major-General F. Steele, U. S. Volunteers, to raise a regiment of volunteer infantry, for one year's service.

In reply I have respectfully to inform you that the authorization referred to was granted without the authority of the War Department and the force recruited there-under was never accepted or recruited by the War Department into the service of the United States. Upon the application and report of Captain Swain, superintendent volunteer recruiting service for the State of Arkansas, that officer was authorized by telegram, dated April 27, 1864, to enlist the men for three years, and date musters back to cover twelve months term.

The records of this office fail to furnish any information of the force, as it was never mustered into the United States service or mustered for pay.

The statement that there were three hundred (300) men enlisted is that from the report of Captain Swain. No returns have been made to this office showing that the force, or any part of it, elected to enter the service for three (3) years under the formal authorization of the War Department through the Provost-Marshal General of the

United States, dated April 27, 1864, hereinbefore referred to, and copy herewith* enclosed.

There is, therefore, under existing laws no way in which payment to the force in question can be made.

I am, sir, very respectfully, your obedient servant,

THOMAS M. VINCENT,
Assistant Adjutant-General.

WAR DEPARTMENT, ADJUTANT-GENERAL'S OFFICE,
Washington, January 19, 1870.

Hon. LOGAN H. ROOTS, M. C.:
House of Representatives:

SIR: Referring to your verbal requests for information, &c., relative to the organization and services of the 4th Arkansas Mounted Infantry Volunteers, Hon. Elisha Baxter, recruiting officer, I have the honor to inform you that the following information is required and deemed necessary in connection with action looking to the recognition of certain members of said regiment:

At what posts, or whereat, did the men serve?

If service was not at military posts, but detached, what was the character of said detached service?

What supplies, if any, were issued to the men?

From whom, or from what depots or posts, were the supplies obtained?

Were the men kept together in bodies, or were they permitted to go and do as they saw fit; that is, were they at liberty to go to their homes and other places at their pleasure?

If the men, or any of them, were in battle, name it and the circumstances, &c.

The official records of this office afford some evidence of service, but the foregoing is deemed essential to complete the records.

I am, sir, very respectfully, your obedient servant,

THOMAS M. VINCENT,
Assistant Adjutant-General.

The following is a report on joint resolution (H. R. 121), January 19, 1870, providing for the payment of the 4th Arkansas Mounted Infantry:

WAR DEPARTMENT, ADJUTANT-GENERAL'S OFFICE,
Washington, January 26, 1870.

Major-General F. Steele, U. S. Volunteers, authorized, October 23, 1863, the 4th Arkansas Mounted Infantry to be recruited for twelve (12) months' service. There was no law for such an authorization, and it was given without the sanction of the War Department. By telegram from the superintendent of the volunteer recruiting service for Arkansas, dated April 20, 1864, it was reported that upwards of three hundred men—enlisted for twelve months—were at Batesville, Arkansas, and that the intended colonel (Baxter), who had been authorized to recruit the regiment, gave assurance that the said men would "enlist for three years if their muster can be dated back to time of original enlistment and they can now receive pay and benefits arising from a muster of such date." This was the first notice the department had of the organization. Upon the matter being submitted to the Secretary of War, he decided that the "three hundred (300) men at Batesville may be enlisted for three (3) years and musters dated back to cover twelve (12) months' term. In so doing no right or claim will be granted for any other bounty than the one hundred dollars ($100) provided by act of 1861," and the decision was communicated by telegram, dated April 27, 1864.

It appears that the men did not accept the conditions and did not enlist as authorized by the Secretary of War. It seems, however, that they rendered some service, in good faith, as attested by Major-General Steele's department return, bearing as follows:

	Commissioned officers.	Enlisted men.
For January, 1864	5	222
" February, "	1	270
" March, "	1	331
" April, "	1	383
" May, "	1	394

After May the force, which was never even organized into companies, ceased to be accounted for.

The proposed joint resolution has been altered as indicated in the copy herewith, so as to carefully guard the interests of the United States, and is recommended as the form under which relief shall be extended.

E. D. TOWNSEND,
Adjutant-General.

JOINT RESOLUTION, Providing for the payment of the Fourth Arkansas Mounted Infantry Volunteers.*

Resolved by the Senate and House of Representatives of the United States of America in Congress assembled, That the Secretary of War [be, and he is hereby, directed immediately] upon the possession [by him] of evidence of service *which to him may seem satisfactory, is hereby directed* to cause to be investigated the claims of the forces known as the Fourth Arkansas Mounted Infantry, *enlisted for 12 months* [organized] under the [orders] *authority dated October* 23, 1863, of Major-General Frederick Steele, in Northwestern Arkansas [in eighteen hundred and sixty-four, and if he find *and if he finds* the troops were organized under authority of the United States officer in command of the Department of Arkansas and], *the troops* performed actual service, he shall *cause* [pay] the officers and soldiers thereof *to be paid* at the same rates for actual services rendered while absent from their homes as was allowed by law to other volunteer forces in the military service at the same *time, and estimating the amount due the said force the officers and non-commissioned officers thereof shall be paid under the mustering regulations of the Army in force at the time the regiment was under recruitment* [date], and no allowance shall be made for any troops who did not perform actual military service in full co-operation and subject to the orders of the United States authorities: *Provided, That no payment shall be made for any time after the date the enlisted men declined to enlist for three years, with a muster dated back to cover the 12 months term, as tendered by the War Department, by telegram through the Pro. Mar. General dated April 27, 1864.*

BATESVILLE, ARKANSAS, *March* 29, 1870.
To the Hon. SECRETARY OF WAR,
Washington, D. C.:

DEAR SIR: I have just been informed by the Senators and Representatives from this State that a law has passed authorizing the payment of the officers and men of the 4th Arkansas Mounted Infantry. I have supposed that it would be necessary for you, in your official capacity, to procure forms and rules for the production of proof by the officers and men of said regt. If so, you will confer a special favor by causing to be forwarded to me, at your earliest convenience, all such documents and information as will enable the parties interested to apply understandingly for their pay.

Humbly trusting that you will not be annoyed with this request,

I have the honor to be, very respectfully,

ELISHA BAXTER,
Provisional Col. of the 4th Arkansas Mounted Infantry.

WAR DEPARTMENT,
ADJUTANT-GENERAL'S OFFICE,
Washington, D. C., April 16, 1870.

ELISHA BAXTER, Esq.,
Late Provisional Colonel,
4th Arkansas Mounted Infantry,
Batesville, Arkansas:

SIR: Referring to your letter of the 29th ultimo, to the Secretary of War, in regard to the joint resolution of March 18, 1870, providing for the payment of the 4th Arkansas Mounted Infantry Volunteers, I have respectfully to invite your attention to a letter [copy herewith†] dated January 19, 1870, to the Hon. L. H. Roots, M.C., to which no reply has been received. Prior to further action by this office, the information called for in that letter must be furnished, as it is essentially necessary to final action by the War Department.

In addition, all rolls (muster and descriptive, muster for pay or muster in) that can be produced or referred to, and all enlistment papers that can be produced or referred to, should be forwarded or pointed out, so that this office may have access to them. If those records cannot now be produced or referred to, then lists of names, with dates of enlistment, by whom recruited or enrolled, where enlisted or enrolled, when

---

* The portions inclosed in brackets are erased in the original; the new matter inserted is printed in italics.
† See page 6, *ante.*

and where disbanded or discharged, should be made and sent forward. An early compliance with the requirements of this, and the letter of January 19, 1870, to Mr. Roots, is requested.

Very respectfully, your obedient servant,

T. M. VINCENT,
Assistant Adjutant-General.

U. S. HOUSE OF REPRESENTATIVES,
COMMITTEE ON PACIFIC RAILROADS,
Washington, D. C., May 10th, 1870.

Gen'l E. D. TOWNSEND,
Adj't Gen'l, U. S. A.:

Will you be kind enough to furnish me a full statement of what co. & field and staff rolls are already on file in your office of the 4th Arkansas M't'd Inf't'y Vols.?

I am, resp'y,

LOGAN H. ROOTS,
M. C., Ark.

WAR DEPARTMENT, ADJUTANT-GENERAL'S OFFICE,
Washington, D. C., May 14th, 1870.

Hon. LOGAN H. ROOTS, M. C.,
House of Representatives:

SIR: Referring to your letter of May 10th, asking what company and field and staff rolls of the 4th Arkansas Mounted Infantry are on file in this office, I have the honor to inform you that before the department can give any information in regard to the case, or take any further action in it, a reply will be necessary to the letter to you dated January 19, 1870, asking certain information, and also to one to Elisha Baxter, Esq., dated April 16th, 1870 (copy herewith*), asking for some additional information as to enlistment papers, muster and descriptive, and muster for pay rolls.

As soon as the information required by these letters is furnished, suitable action can be promptly taken in the matter.

I am, sir, very respectfully, your obedient servant,

E. D. TOWNSEND,
Adj.tant-General.

BATESVILLE, ARKANSAS, *June 21st, 1870.*

Gen. THOMAS M. VINCENT,
Ass't Adjutant-General, U. S. A., Washington, D. C.:

GENERAL: I have the honor to transmit to your department a roll† of the company under my command in the 4th Regiment of Arkansas Mounted Infantry Volunteers, in compliance with instructions from your office of April 16th, 1870, to Elisha Baxter, late provisional colonel of said regiment.

Very respectfully, your ob'd't serv't,

JAMES E. CONNER,
Late Capt. Co. C, 4th Ark. M't'd Inf., per Wm. A. Inman.

BATESVILLE, ARKANSAS, *June 28th, 1870.*

To the Hon. the SECRETARY OF WAR,
Washington, D. C.:

SIR: In response to yours of the —— last, and a similar letter to Hon. Logan H. Roots with regard to the status of the 4th Arkansas Mounted Infantry, I have the honor to transmit herewith the sworn statement of myself and of as many of the provisional officers of said regiment as are accessible to me, which I hope will answer the ends contemplated by you. Absence from home and the difficulty of obtaining the signatures of the different officers of the regt. has delayed this communication till now.

Simultaneously herewith I mail to your address a copy of the report of the Adjutant-Gen'l of Arkansas for the years 1861 to 1866, and respectfully refer you to pages 246 to 250, inclusive, for the only published history of this regt. extant.

With high regard, I am, very truly, your obedient servant,

ELISHA BAXTER.

* See page 7, *ante.*
† Copy of roll transmitted herein, marked A.

STATE OF ARKANSAS,
County of Independence, ss:

I, Elisha Baxter, late provisional colonel of the 4th Arkansas (Mounted Infantry) on oath state that I did on the 23rd day of October, A. D., 1863, receive from the hands of Maj. Gen'l F. Steele, then commanding the U. S. forces in the State of Arkansas, an order of which the following is an exact copy, the original of which, and sundry other orders pertaining to the regt., are now in my possession and are held subject to the inspection of the War Department.

HEADQUARTERS ARMY OF ARKS.,
Little Rock, Arks., Oct. 23d, 1863.

Elisha Baxter, of Batesville, Independence County, State of Arkansas, is hereby authorized to raise a Regiment of Infantry to be mustered into the United States service for the term of one year or during the war, if not sooner discharged. The headquarters for the recruiting will be at Batesville, Independence County, and all persons recruiting for said regiment will be governed by the regulations for the recruiting service, and orders from War Department, Department of Missouri, and these headquarters.

Mr. Baxter will report to these headquarters for such instructions as he may require.

By order of Maj. Gen'l F. Steele.

A. H. RYAN,
Capt. and A. D. C.

And further, in pursuance of said order, I did, on or about the 24th day of October, A. D. 1863, proceed under the escort of the 3rd Missouri Cavalry, Lieut. Col. Black, commanding, to the town of Jacksonport, in the vicinity of Batesville, and enter at once upon my duties as recruiting officer, in which capacity I remained at Jacksonport until the 29th day of December, A. D. 1863, keeping such men as I then had in camps, obeying and carrying out to the best of my ability all orders of my superior officers, and drawing rations in the regular manner from the commissary department at Jacksonport.

The 3rd Missouri Cavalry being then ordered to Little Rock, I reported with such men as I then had on hand to Col. R. R. Livingston, of the 1st Nebraska Cavalry, at Batesville, when I was, by Col. Livingston, assigned to quarters for myself, officers, and men; drew arms, clothing, and rations for my command; performed and caused my officers and men to perform all the duties incumbent upon me as a soldier, furnishing regularly from this time on details for fatigue and picket duty; and in all respects received and held myself amenable for the execution of such orders as were made by Col. Livingston, or any of my superior officers, the same as if I had been regularly and duly commissioned colonel of the regiment, until the 12th day of May, A. D. 1864, when I was relieved from the command by the following order, to wit:

[Special Order, No. 91.]

HEADQUARTERS DEP'T OF ARKANSAS,
Little Rock, May 3rd, 1864.

VIII. Hon. E. Baxter, recruiting officer for the 4th Arkansas Mounted Infantry, having been elected to the Senate of the United States from the State of Arkansas, is hereby relieved from duty with that regiment, and will turn over his command and all orders and instructions he may have received relating to the organization of the same to Capt. S. A. Baxter [properly T. A. Baxter], 4th Arkansas Mounted Infantry, subject to the approval of the War Department.

By order of Maj. Gen'l F. Steele.

W. D. GREENE,
Ass't Adj't Gen'l.

Hon. E. BAXTER,
Pro. Col. & Rec. Officer, 4th Ark's Mounted Infantry.

And in pursuance of the foregoing order, I did, on the 12th day of May, A. D. 1864, issue the following order, to wit:

[Special Order No. 2.]

HEADQUARTERS 4TH ARK'S M'T'D INF. VOL'S,
Batesville, May 12, 1864.

I. By Special Order No. 91, dated headquarters Department of Arkansas, I am relieved from duty, and required to assign the command together with all authority in me vested to Capt. T. A. Baxter, senior capt. of the command. From this date Capt. Baxter will assume command of the 4th Ark's Inf't'y, and will be obeyed and respected accordingly.

II. He will render forthwith proper accounts for all ordnance, ordnance stores, camp & garrison equipage, and quartermaster stores belonging to the regiment.

III. The col. com'd'g takes this occasion to express his earnest regrets at his separation from the reg't, and returns his cordial thanks to the officers and men of his command for the prompt and diligent efforts they have made under the most embarrassing circumstances to restore the flag of our country.

III. He desires also to return his thanks to Col. R. R. Livingston, com'd'g dist. N. E. Ark's, and to the officers and men of his command for their kind and courteous bearing during his connexion with them in the military service.

By order of E. Baxter, col. and recruiting officer, 4th Ark's Inf't'y.

WM. H. ROSA, Act. Adj't.

Thereby turning over to Capt. T. A. Baxter the entire command.

And I do further state that the officers and men under my command during the time above mentioned drew all their necessary supplies of arms, clothing, and rations from the posts of Jacksonport and Batesville (principally from the latter). The services performed were either at one of the above-mentioned posts, or under orders emanating therefrom.

The men were kept together as other U. S. troops, and were fully supplied with camp and garrison equipage from the post of Batesville.

Men from my command were in quite a number of engagements and skirmishes.

Fifty men, detailed from my regiment under Captain T. A. Baxter, surprised the enemy, seventy-five strong, at Lunenburg, in Izard County, about the 10th day of January, 1864, drove them from their position, killed one, wounded two, took five prisoners, several horses, and several stand of arms, with the loss of but one man.

A detail of twenty-five men from my command, under Lt. John W. Ayres, reported to Capt. Castle, of the 11th Mo. Cavalry, on the 18th of Feb'y, as a foraging party, and on the morning of the 19th they were surprised at Waugh's, in Independence County, by Major Rutherford of the rebel army, with two hundred men. A fierce engagement ensued; the Federal forces were driven from their position, with the loss of their entire train; Capt. Castle, & two men of the 11th Mo., one from the 4th Arkansas, and a negro killed; several wounded; and five prisoners from the 4th Arkansas, four of whom were refused the right to exchange, and held for court-martial upon the pretext that they were, by virtue of the conscript law of the rebellious States, deserters from the rebel army, but upon being assured by me (with the permission of Colonel Livingston) that we would retaliate if said men were punished, they were afterwards paroled and returned to camp.

On or about the 20th of Feb'y, I was ordered by Col. Livingston to proceed south of White River in pursuit of Rutherford with such of my own men as could be mounted and one company from the 1st Nebraska Cavalry. I succeeded in mounting only about one hundred of my men. With these, and a company from the 1st Nebraska, under Capt. Ribble, I drove the enemy beyond Red River, captured his conscript camp, consisting of twenty-eight men, a number of horses and arms; and before my return to Batesville, captured a commissary wagon and its contents, and augmented the number of prisoners to about sixty, and the number of horses & mules to about forty.

A considerable detail from the 4th Arkansas was with Lt. Col. Stephens, of the 11th Mo., at Holt's Mill, in Lawrence County, on the 10th of Feb'y, 1864, when a sharp engagement ensued with Freeman's regiment of rebel troops, in which Sergeant Jones, from Co. B, 4th Arks., was wounded.

About the middle of April, 1864, Col. Livingston established district headquarters at Jacksonport, leaving the 4th Arkansas and one company from the 11th Mo. Cavalry in charge of the post of Batesville, Lt. Col. Stephens commanding in the absence of myself (by permission of Col. Livingston) at Little Rock to procure the muster of my reg't. During my connection with the reg't about four hundred men were enlisted, armed, clothed, fed, drilled, and performed service under orders of their superiors in as full and complete a manner as if they had been regularly mustered and the officers duly commissioned. But owing to the almost continual interruption of communication from Batesville and Jacksonport with Little Rock, no mustering officer could be obtained, and the men of my command were never mustered.

And I do further state, as I am informed and believe, that after my connection with the regiment was dissolved, Capt. T. A. Baxter continued to recruit the regiment and command the same until they were disbanded by the following order, to wit:

[Special Order No. 121.]

HEADQUARTERS, DEP'T OF ARKANSAS,
Little Rock, Ark's, June 2, 1864.

[Extract.]

I. The authority heretofore granted for the enlistment for one year of a reg't of Arkansas troops, to be designated the 4th Arkansas Mounted Infantry, not having been confirmed by the War Department, the organization is hereby disbanded.

All quartermaster property and ordnance stores in the possession of the battalion will be turned over to the proper staff officers at De Vall's Bluff.
By order of Maj. Gen'l F. Steele.
W. D. GREENE,
Ass't Adj't Gen'l.

The reg't was accordingly disbanded and the stores turned over as directed, and the papers belonging to Cos. A & B were filed in the office of the Adjutant-Gen'l for the State of Arkansas; the balance of the papers of this command were either destroyed or retained by the individual to whom they belonged.
ELISHA BAXTER.

Subscribed and sworn to before me, W. H. Rosa, notary public for Independence County, Ark's, this 18th day of June, 1870.
WM. H. ROSA, N. P.

STATE OF ARKANSAS,
County of Independence, ss:

I, Taylor A. Baxter, late senior captain of the 4th Arkansas Mounted Infantry, on oath, state that I have carefully examined the foregoing statement of Elisha Baxter and believe the same to be true in all particulars.
TAYLOR A. BAXTER.

Subscribed and sworn to before me, Wm. H. Rosa, notary public for the State of Arkansas, on the 25 day of June, 1870.
WM. H. ROSA, N. P.

STATE OF ARKANSAS,
County of Independence, ss:

I, Moses Ford, late one of the captains of the 4th Arkansas Mounted Infantry, on oath, state that I have carefully examined the foregoing statement of Elisha Baxter, and believe the same to be true.
MOSES FORD.

Subscribed and sworn to before me, Wm. H. Rosa, notary public for the State of Arkansas, this 20th day of June, 1870.
WM. H. ROSA, N. P.

STATE OF ARKANSAS,
County of Independence, ss:

I, William H. Rosa, late acting adjutant of the 4th Arkansas Mounted Infantry, on oath, state that I have carefully examined the foregoing statement of Elisha Baxter, and believe the same to be true.
WM. H. ROSA.

Subscribed and sworn to before me, as judge of the 3d judicial circuit of Arkansas, this 18th day of June, 1870.
ELISHA BAXTER,
Judge, &c.

STATE OF ARKANSAS,
County of Independence, ss:

I, James E. Connor, late one of the captains of the 4th Arkansas Mounted Infautry, on oath, state that I have carefully examined the foregoing statement of Elisha Baxter, and believe the same to be true.
JAMES E. CONNOR.

Subscribed and sworn to before me, Wm. H. Rosa, notary public for the State of Arkansas, this 21st day of June, 1870.
WM. H. ROSA, N. P.

———

TREASURY DEPARTMENT, THIRD AUDITOR'S OFFICE,
March 4, 1871.

SIR: You are respectfully requested to inform this office whether or not the records in your office show that an organization, designated as the 4th Arkansas Mounted Infantry Volunteers, were in the military service of the United States at any time during the war for putting down the rebellion; if so, do the names of Joshua W. Anderson, Absalom W. Bullington, Joseph Lawrence, Henry A. Miller, John S. Mosier, Henry Rensick, Elijah Rogers, and David C. Wolfe appear on any of the rolls of Co. B, C, & D, or any recruit rolls of said regiment or organization. The persons above named have made application for compensation for the value of horses alleged to have been lost while in the military service of the United States during November & December, 1863, and February, 1864.
Very respectfully, your obedient servant,
ALLAN RUTHERFORD,
Auditor.

To the ADJUTANT-GENERAL, U. S. A.,
Washington, D. C.

WAR DEPARTMENT, ADJUTANT-GENERAL'S OFFICE,
Washington, April 3d, 1871.
THIRD AUDITOR, TREASURY DEPARTMENT,
Washington, D. C.:

SIR: I have respectfully to acknowledge the receipt of your letter of the 4th ultimo, stating that certain applications have been presented at your office by persons claiming to have been members of the 4th Arkansas Mounted Infantry for compensation for horses alleged to have been lost by them while in the Army, and requesting to be informed whether the organization referred to is recognized by this office as having been at any time in the service of the United States during the late war.

In reply, I have to inform you that this office is not prepared at this time to give any information in regard to these claims, but so soon as the requirements of the joint resolution approved March 18, 1870, providing for the payment of this force shall have been completed, the information called for will be furnished you as requested.

I am, sir, very respectfully, your obedient servant,
T. M. VINCENT,
Assistant Adjutant-General.

[Law offices of Chipman, Hosmer & Co.   N. P. Chipman, A A. Hosmer, C. D. Gilmore.]
WASHINGTON, D. C., *April 3d,* 1871.
To the ADJUTANT-GENERAL, U. S. A.:

GENERAL: At the request of Hon. L. H. Roots, of Arkansas, we submit herewith rolls* of Co's B, C, D, and E, and of the field and staff of the Fourth Regiment Arkansas Mounted Infantry.

If further rolls are required or other information as to the matter, we have to request that Mr. Roots be addressed in reference thereto at Batesville, Ark.

Resp'ly,
CHIPMAN, HOSMER & CO.

WAR DEPARTMENT, ADJUTANT-GENERAL'S OFFICE,
Washington D. C., April 28th, 1871.
To the SECOND AUDITOR OF THE TREASURY,
Washington, D. C.:

SIR: An investigation is about to be had under the orders of the Secretary of War, in connection with the evidence of service submitted by members the 4th Arkansas Mounted Infantry, under the provisions of the joint resolutions approved March 18, 1870. As necessary thereto, I have the honor to request that you will cause to be forwarded to this office such rolls of that organization as may have been filed in your office, together with such submitted evidence as you may deem necessary to secure a careful comparison of records with a view of establishing complete and satisfactory evidence of service.

I am, sir, very respectfully, your obedient servant,
E. D. TOWNSEND,
Adjutant-General.
[Endorsement.]
TREASURY DEPARTMENT, SECOND AUDITOR'S OFFICE,
May 4th, 1871.

Respectfully returned to the Adjutant-General with the information that there are no rolls of the 4th Arkansas Mounted Volunteers on file in this office, and no evidence of service that has been submitted by members of that organization.

E. B. FRENCH,
Auditor.
By D. A. P.

[Law offices of Chipman, Hosmer & Co.   N. P. Chipman, A. A. Hosmer, C. D. Gilmore.]
WASHINGTON, D. C , *July 6th,* 1871.
To the ADJUTANT-GENERAL, U. S. A.:

GENERAL: We have the honor to state that, in support of claims filed by us in office of the Hon. 2d Auditor, we sent to your office some time since rolls of various companies in the Fourth Arkansas Mounted Inf'y, and to ask if any further rolls are required to secure the usual reports from your office, on which the Auditor makes payments.

Respectfully,
CHIPMAN, HOSMER, & Co.

WAR DEPARTMENT, ADJUTANT-GENERAL'S OFFICE,
Washington, July 14, 1871.
Messrs. CHIPMAN, HOSMER and CO.,
Attorneys, &c., Washington, D. C.:

GENTLEMEN: Referring to your letter of the 6th int., requesting to be informed what additional information is required by this office to secure action on the claims of members of the 4th Arkansas Mounted Infantry Volunteers, under the joint resolution approved March 18, 1870, I have respectfully to inform you that the following is deemed necessary to secure the action referred to:

1. A certified roll of Company A.
2d. Please state at what posts or whereat did the men serve? If service was not at military posts, and detached, what was character of said detached service?
3d. What supplies, if any, were issued to the men?
4th. From whom or from what depots or posts were the supplies obtained.
5th. Were the men kept in bodies, or were they permitted to go and do as they saw fit; that is, were they at liberty to go to their homes and other places at their pleasure?
6th. If the men, or any of them, were in battle, name it, together with such evidence of actual service as may be obtained.

I am gentlemen, very respectfully, your obedient servant,
T. M. VINCENT,
Asst. Adj't-General.

[Law offices Chipman, Hosmer & Co. N. P. Chipman, A. A. Hosmer, C. D. Gilmore.]

WASHINGTON, D. C., *Oct.* 16, 1871.
To the ADJUTANT-GEN., U. S. A.:

GENERAL: We have the honor to enclose *rolls of Co. A, 4th Arkansas Mounted Infantry, which, we believe, completes the evidence required to complete the records of that regiment.

The letter from your office requiring this evidence is mislaid.

Resp'ly,
CHIPMAN, HOSMER & CO.

WAR DEPARTMENT, ADJUTANT-GENERAL'S OFFICE,
Washington, D. C., November 9th, 1871.
Messrs. CHIPMAN, HOSMER & CO.,
Attorneys at Law, Washington, D. C.:

GENTLEMEN: Referring to the papers and rolls submitted by you July 6, and October 16, 1871, in the claim of the 4th Arkansas Mounted Volunteers, for recognition and pay under the act approved March 18, 1870, I have respectfully to inform you that in order to intelligent action on the same prior to consideration by the Secretary of War, it will be necessary for you to file in this office powers of attorney in each claim, all orders under which the troops served, as alleged, and all memoranda, correspondence, and other data accompanying the several claims and rolls as prepared in your office.

All statements which you may secure to support or accompany the rolls must be under oath.

I am, gentlemen, very respectfully, your obedient servant,
THOMAS M. VINCENT,
Assistant Adjutant-General.

[Law offices of Hosmer & Co. A. A. Hosmer, C. D. Gilmore.]

WASHINGTON, D. C., *Nov.* 11, 1871.
To the ADJUTANT-GENERAL:

In reply to your letter of the 9th instant, concerning the recognition of the 4th Arkansas Mounted Infantry and the payment of its members, we have the honor to state that in most of the claims filed by us there are "enlistment papers" in the regular form prescribed by the War Department, on which are also endorsed by the different company commanders the dates of discharges, and that wherever such papers are not furnished there are filed affidavits of commanders of companies giving dates of enlistment and discharges, and proof of loss of enlistment papers; there is also in each case filed by us a power of attorney from the claimant. The claims filed by us are in the office of the Second Auditor of the Treasury, and a list of them is herewith submitted.

*Marked G.

Colonel Baxter informs us that he has forwarded to the War Department, or lost, the orders under which the regiment served. The order organizing the regiment was issued by General Steele in November, 1863. We forward herewith "report of the A. G. of Arkansas," on pages 246–250 of which are certain orders, lists, memoranda, &c., and which, with papers already filed by us, contain all our information in relation to the regiment.

Respectfully,

CHIPMAN, HOSMER & CO.

Enlisted men, Company A.

Arnold, Ralph.
Burgess, Leroy.
Blivens, Alcana D.
Bryant, William H.
Berry. Spencer.
Bell, William W.
Baker, W. H.
Churchwell, William P.
Corten, John W.
Covenstone, Andrew J.
Chamnees, N. C.
Davis, Elijah.
Evans, John T.
Ellis, William W.
Evans, Thomas J.

Ferguson, Ellis A.
Fuller, Calvin J.
Holt, Elijah.
Holt, Pleasant.
Hendricks, J. K. P.
Harris, Frank.
King, Lewis T.
Kinglet, John J.
Lemons, John T.
Lemons, Josephus.
Lemons, Samuel.
Massey, James D.
Mathews, William I.
Meeks, R. D.

Mathews, Jesse C.
Nunnally, William.
Noblin, Thomas.
Pyland, John E.
Southard, Andrew J.
Snodgrass, George D.
Slayton, W. T.
Sherville, Andrew J.
Scruggs, John B.
Teel, Andrew J.
Toney, William.
Watson, James A.
Wilson, James K. P.
Wilson, Geo., M. D.

Enlisted men, Company B.

Anderson, Isaac S.
Anderson, Joshua A.
Barber, A. A.
Ford, Wm. R.
Goad, George W.
Goad, James J.
Gifford, J. E.
Gire, Wm. H.

Lane, Bird.
McLeod, Neill.
McGee, J. K. P.
Mobley, Calvin.
Price, L. C.
Price, J. G.
Pinkerton, H. G.

Smith John E.
Simpson, A. A.
Scroggins, G. A.
Swick, George A.
Tindall, R. P.
Wolfe. John.
Whitlow, Stephen C.

Enlisted men, Company C.

Bullington, A. W.
Ball, C. M.
Ball, H. A.
Bishop, Wm. C.
Ball, Warren G.
Barnwell, G. W.
Ball, Geo. W.
Brewer, J. A.
Crigler, Wm. H.
Chandler, B. F.
Chandler, S. K.
Conner, Isaac.
Cochrane, Wm. H.

Evans, David B.
Gillam, Harris.
Goode, Benj. F.
Green, J. M.
Harvey, Benj.
Hafstedler, Jacob.
Harrold, M. B.
Harley, M. M.
Jackson, Benj. F.
Jackson, James S.
King, Francis M.
King, Wm. H.
King, H. C.

Laboss, John.
Lawrence, Joseph.
Lewallen, M. U.
Morrow, Wm.
Nichols, Sam'l A.
Palston, Jno. N.
Perkins, James.
Ross, Joseph.
Slayton, Green D.
Turner, Lewis.
Winston, J. F.
Young, Henry H.
Young, John N.

Enlisted men, Company D.

Bundy, Wm. H.
Brooks, James U.
Blue, Joseph.
Brown, Neal S.
Blagg, Saml.
Cunningham, Wm. T.
Cochrane, H.
Davis, Jas. C. C.
Johnson, E. B.

Lack, Wm. J.
Martin, Daniel.
Miller, Henry A.
Moser, C. A.
Mason, Berrille A.
Moser, John J.
Mosier, Jacob.
Ray, Jno. T.
Runsick, Henry.

Sipe, Jacob S.
Smith, Enoch.
Sipe, Rufus.
Smith, Leander D.
Sipe, Wm. S.
Swope, John.
Young, Andrew J.

Officers and miscellaneous.

In the following cases of enlisted men our records do not show the compampany to which the soldier belonged :

Greenway, Jas. T.	Miser, John R.	Snoblin, Thomas.
Grimes, DavidH.	Noblin, S. J.	Bundy, Ransom C.
Hendricks, Isaac B.	Noblin, Cullen.	Beckham, Reddy.

WAR DEPARTMENT, ADJUTANT-GENERAL'S OFFICE,
Washington, November 11, 1871.

ADJUTANT-GENERAL OF ARKANSAS,
Little Rock, Arkansas:

GENERAL: Referring to the act approved March 18, 1870, for the relief of the 4th Arkansas Mounted Infantry, I have respectfully to request that you will please forward to this office at your earliest convenience the rolls of that organization, memoranda, correspondence, the orders under which the troops served, and all other data or records that may be on file in your office, in order to intelligent action on the same prior to consideration by the Secretary of War.

This office is informed that the records called for were deposited in your office on the disbanding of the organization, and they are indispensably necessary to this office prior to final action.

I am, sir, very respectfully, your obedient servant,

T. M. VINCENT,
Asst. Adjt.-General.

ADJUTANT-GENERAL'S OFFICE, STATE OF ARKANSAS,
Little Rock, January 12th, 1872.

Major THOMAS M. VINCENT,
Assistant Adjutant-General, U. S. A., Washington, D. C. :

SIR: Herewith I respectfully forward all rolls,* orders, memoranda, correspondence,† &c., relating to the 4th Arkansas Mounted Infantry, on file in this office. The roll of the field and staff, Capt. Harris' and Fond's companies, are unofficial, and were filed by Ex. Adjutant Martin Beam, about two years ago.

I have the honor to be, very respectfully, your ob'd't servant,

KEYES DANFORTH,
Adjutant-General.

1.

[Special Orders, No. 91.]

HEADQUARTERS DEPARTMENT OF ARKANSAS,
Little Rock, Arkansas, May 3d, 1864.

VIII. Hon. E. Baxter, recruiting officer for the 4th Arkansas Mounted Infantry, having been elected to the Senate of the United States, from the State of Arkansas, is hereby relieved from duty with that regt. and will turn over his command and all orders and instructions he may have received relating to the organization of the same to Capt. T. A. Baxter, 4th Arks. Mounted Infantry, subject to the approval of the War Department.

By order of Maj. Gen'l F. Steele.

O. D. GREENE,
Assistant Adjutant-Gen'l.

2.

[Special Orders, No. 121—Extract.]

HEADQUARTERS DEP'T OF ARKS.,
Little Rock, Arks., June 2d, 1864.

II. The authority heretofore granted for the enlistment for one year of a regt. of Arkansas troops, to be designated the 4th Arkansas Mounted Infantry, not having been confirmed by the War Department, the organization is hereby disbanded.

---

* Marked H. I. J. K. and L.   † Numbered, respectively, 1, 2, 3, 4, and 5.

All quartermaster's property and ordnance stores in the possession of the battalion will be turned over to the proper staff officers at Devall's Bluff.

By order of Maj. Genl. F. Steele.

W. D. GREEN,
Assistant Adjt. Genl.

3.

CAMP 4TH ARK. INF. VOLS.,
Du Vall's Bluff, Ark., June 4th, 1864.

I certify on honor that Martin Beem, of Alton, Illinois, has done duty in this command as first lieutenant and adjutant since the first day of January, 1864, & was discharged with the regiment by Special Order No. 121, dated June 2nd, 1864, Dep't of Arkansas.

T. A. BAXTER,
Capt. Com'dg Reg't 4th Ark. Inf. Vols.

[Endorsement.]

HEADQ'RS 1ST REGT. NEB. CAVALRY,
De Vall's Bluff, Ark., June 4th, 1864.

I take pleasure in testifying to the ability and zeal of the within named officer, and trust that government will remunerate him for services rendered in 4th Ark. Inf. Vols., which was raised and served in the Dist. of N. E. Arkansas while I commanded it.

R. R. LIVINGSTON,
Col. 1st Regt. Neb. Cav'ly.

WASHINGTON, D. C., *Ap'l 17, '69.*

I take pleasure in certifying to my knowledge of the services of Martin Beem as adjutant of the 4th Arkansas Mounted Infantry Vols.

This regiment was recruited and served in the Dist. of N. E. Ark. with my command; & when not disabled from service he was constantly on duty. As an officer he was active and efficient, with ample ability and experience to fill almost any position in the Army; and his merit and previous services, in my judgment, made him highly deserving a better rank.

His disability, as certified to by Maj. Wm. McLelland, Med. Director N. E. Ark., is familiar to myself & other officers with whom he was associated.

Very resp'y, &c.,
(Sgd.)

TOM MAJORS,
Late Maj. 1st Neb. V. V. Cav.

Having served with Maj. Majors, & being personally acquainted with Martin Beem, I cheerfully vouch for the foregoing statement.

Signed

T. W. TIPTON,
U. S. Senator (Nebraska).

During the period referred to by Maj. Thos. Major, of the 1st Neb. Cav'ly, I was Asst. Adj't Gen'l of the dist. of N. E. Arkansas, & was constantly in business communication with Lieut. Beem, then adj't of the 4th Ark. M. Inf. Vols., and found him a faithful and competent officer, always prompt & accurate in furnishing the reports and returns of his command, as prescribed by regulations, & a constant applicant for the post of honor in the many scouting expeditions we were obliged to send thro' a region of country infested by the forces of the enemy, exceeding, if concentrated, the whole of our combined numerical force in strength.

The services he rendered under these circumstances justly entitled him to the increase of rank which would undoubtedly have been his reward had the organization of which he was a member been continued in service.

HENRY C. FILLEBROWN,
Late Capt. & A. A. G., U. S. V., A. A. G. Dist. N. E. Ark.

[Special Order No. 91—Extract.]

H'DQ'RS DEP'T OF ARK.,
Little Rock, Ark., May 3d, 1864.

8. Hon. E. Baxter, recruiting officer for the 4th Ark. M. I. V., having been elected to the Senate of the U. S. from the State of Arkansas, is hereby relieved from duty with that regiment, & will turn over his command & all orders & instructions he

may have received relating to the organization of the same to Capt. T. A. Baxter, 4th Ark. M. I. V., subject to the approval of the War Dep't.

By order of Maj. Gen. F. Steele.

W. D. GREEN,
A. A. G.

Official.

JNO. F. LACEY,
A. A. G.

Personally appeared before me, Martin Beem (who is personally known by me) who, being duly sworn, says that the foregoing are true copies of papers and endorsements now on file in the War Dep't at Washington.

MARTIN BEEM.

Sworn to and subscribed before me this twenty-sixth day of August, A. D. 1870, at Little Rock, Ark.

[SEAL.]

GEO. W. CLARK,
Notary Public, Pulaski Co., Ark.

———

4.

LITTLE ROCK, ARKS., *June 10th*, 1865.

Col. A. W. BISHOP,
Adj't-General, Arks.:

DEAR SIR: Yours of the 7th of June requesting information for official purposes as to the authority for and manner of recruiting the 4th (instead of first) Arkansas Mounted Infantry, has been received.

The 4th Arkansas Mounted Infantry was recruited and commanded by me, from some time in Novb. A. D. 1863, until the 12th of May, A. D. 1864, under authority of an order from Maj. Gen. Steele, authorizing me to recruit a regt. of men, for the United States service for twelve months, the precise date or language of which I cannot now give or quote, since the original is filed with Hon. Henry Wilson, as chairman of the Military Committee of the U. S. Senate, with a view to induce favorable legislation in behalf of the regt., and the only copy that I have retained is with my family in Illinois.

During the time I was in command of the regiment I enlisted about four hundred men, mostly at the town of Batesville, in the N. E. portion of the State.

After the date of the order referred to, I obtained verbal permission of Maj. Gen. Steele to mount the men and report them as mounted infantry, which, by referance to a copy of the order relieving me, herewith inclosed, will more fully appear.

In consequence of the interruption of communication between the headqr's of the dep't and Batesville, an authorized mustering officer could not be procured during the time I was connected with the command.

By reference to the copy of order herewith inclosed it will also appear that on being relieved I was required to turn the command over to Capt. T. A. Baxter as senior capt. of the regt. (which was done), who, I have no doubt, will take great pleasure in furnishing you any information in his possession in regard to the regt. since the date of the order relieving me.

Respectfully yours,

E. BAXTER,
Provisional Col. 4th Ark. M. Inf'vy.

P. S.—I also send you herewith a copy of an order disbanding the regiment.

E. B., *Col., &c.*

———

5.

CHICAGO, *April 1st*, 1870.

Gen. KEYES DANFORTH,
Adj't Genl., &c., Little Rock:

DEAR GEN'L :—I have the honor to send you herewith copies of some papers I have in my possession which will testify to my services as adjutant of the 4th Arkansas Mounted Infantry.

In the absence of all official records, I have thought it best to send this additional evidence, with a request that you file the same in your office to rebut the claims of any other who may be urged or apply to you for your recognition.

Not knowing but these would be superfluous, I have not sworn to their being *verbatim* copies of the originals now in my possession, but can do so if required to establish my claim.

I am, very respectfully, your obed't serv't,

MARTIN BEEM,
128 *N. State.*

S. Ex. 59——2

[General Orders, No. 79.]

HEADQUARTERS, DEPARTMENT OF THE MISSOURI,
St. Louis, Mo., August 4th, 1863.

The following instructions from the War Department are published for the information and guidance of all concerned:

WAR DEPARTMENT, ADJUTANT-GENERAL'S OFFICE,
Washington, D. C, July 29, 1863.

MAJOR-GENERAL J. M. SCHOFIELD,
Commanding Department of the Missouri, St. Louis, Mo. :

GENERAL: I have the honor to acknowledge the receipt of your letter of the 10th inst., in relation to the appointment of officers of Arkansas troops. In reply, I am directed to inform you that the appointments will be made by this department upon the recommendation of the general commanding the department in which the troops are serving. No officer will enter upon duty until the recommendation has been approved and notification of the same received.

I am, General, very respectfully, your obed't serv't,

THOMAS M. VINCENT,
Assistant Adjutant-General.

II. Officers now serving in Arkansas regiments, companies of batteries, and who have not received official notification of their appointments by the War department, or of the approval by the War Department of their appointments, will not be considered in service until such appointment shall be made.

Rosters of the officers of all such regiments, companies and batteries, certified and approved by their commanders, and all intermediate commanders, will be sent without delay to these headquarters.

III. All persons in this department having authority from any source to raise Arkansas troops, will send without delay to these headquarters certified copies of such authority, together with a full report of the progress made in recruiting and organizing troops.

Until such authority shall be received at department headquarters and approved, it will not be regarded as valid.

By command of Major-General SCHOFIELD :

C. W. MARSH,
Assistant Adjutant-General.

Additional evidence submitted by Hosmer & Co., attorneys.

PLATTSMOUTH, NEB., *Feb'y 5, '72.*

Messrs. HOSMER & CO.,
Washington, D. C. :

GENTLEMEN: Your favor 30th ult. relative to Col. Elijah Baxter's 4th Ark. Mounted Infantry, is rec'd.

In reply I would state that I organized the regiment under orders of Major-Gen'l Jno. M. Schofield, at that time com'd'g Dept. of Missouri.

The arms were supplied to me by Col. Callender at the St. Louis Arsenal, & taken overland on my trains from Rolla, Mo., to Batesville, Ark., where the regiment was organized.

Detachments of the 4th Ark. M't'd Inf't'y were frequently employed by my orders; on some occasions they had men wounded & captured. I recollect one instance on White River when Capt. Baxter, a brother of the Col., was acting as escort to a forage train, when attacked by one George Rutherford and band, resulting in a defeat of Baxter.

The papers belonging to No. E. Dis't of Arkansas, when I left them, on veteran furlough, were turned over to Adj't-Gen'l's office at Little Rock, & should be available to prove service. While I cannot after this lapse of time designate any particulars, I can say that I ordered detachments of the 4th Ark. M't'd Inf't'y on duty frequently, & that the whole force of that reg't was doing duty under my orders in the N. E. Dis't of Ark., where they were clothed & subsisted the same as other troops, and did precisely the same service.

Yours, respectfully,

ROBT. R. LIVINGSTON.

198 W. Madison, Chicago,
Feb'y 16th, '72.

Mes. Chipman, H. & Co.,
Wash., D. C.:

Gents: A short note just rec'd from the Hon. Logan H. Root at W., suggests to me to write you & "give you any help, information, or suggestion" which will help the payment of the 4th Ark. Mounted Inf.

I don't know the cause of the delay of the payment of that command "upon proper proof of service." The history of the reg't must be familiar to you. Its organization & muster out was informal; but that it rendered good service, Gen'l R. R. Livingston, formerly Col. 1st Nebraska Cav'l'y, & commander of the Dist. N. E. Ark., at the time of the organization & service of these men can, & 1 think would, cheerfully testify.

So could Gen'l Steele, if living. Gen'l Livingston is now surveyor-gen'l (I believe) of Nebraska, & living at Plattsmouth, Neb., or at Omaha. A letter to either place would reach him. I don't know what I can do more to expedite matters. If any general affidavit of its service, organization, discharge, &c., will avail aught, I shall be glad to make it or do anything else to help those who did service to get the little pay that is now & has been so long due them.

My address is as dated. I presume Col. Root has informed you that I was adjutant of the battalion during its ephemeral existence.

Very respectfully, yours, &c.,

MARTIN BEEM.

The following report was made to the Secretary of War, with a view to decision as to whether or not the various rolls submitted should be accepted as satisfactory evidence of service:

WAR DEPARTMENT, ADJUTANT-GENERAL'S OFFICE,
April 10th, 1872.

Respectfully submitted to the Secretary of War.

A careful investigation of the claim of the 4th Arkansas Mounted Infantry, for recognition and pay, under the act approved March 18th, 1870 (page 62, vol. 16, Statutes at Large), shows that Elisha Baxter, under date of Oct. 23d, 1863, was authorized by General Steele, comd'g headquarters Army of Arkansas, to raise a regiment of infantry for one year, or during the war, but no authority for their being mustered appears.

The returns of the district Northeast Arkansas, based as they were on presence and actual enlistment, report as follows:

Return for Jan'y, 1864, that the 4th Arkansas Mounted Infantry consisted of 5 officers and 222 enlisted men, while the rolls submitted by Chipman, Hosmer & Co., for recognition, report 7 officers and 304 enlisted men.

Return for February, 1864, reports 1 commissioned officer and 270 enlisted men (4 commissioned officers dropped, they having only authority from Colonel Baxter), while the rolls submitted bear the names of 7 officers and 348 enlisted men. Return for March, 1864, reports 1 commissioned officer and 331 enlisted men, while the rolls bear the names of 7 officers and 406 enlisted men.

The return for April, 1864, shows 1 commissioned officer and 383 enlisted men, while the rolls bear the names of 7 officers and 441 enlisted men.

The return for May, 1864, shows 1 commissioned officer and 394 enlisted men, while the rolls referred to show 7 officers and 447 enlisted men.

It is also found that John White, James M. Green, Benj. F. Chastain, and William (M.) Davis, claimants on the rolls herewith, have been heretofore paid as members of the 4th Arkansas Cavalry, and that Wm. Price, another claimant, was paid as a member of the 4th Arkansas Inf't'y.

Again, notations setting forth loss of horses, &c., appear on the rolls submitted, which are not enumerated on the rolls filed in this office, by the adjutant-general of Arkansas.

The name of Albert Legget is reported as having been enlisted by Capt. Connor at Batesville, Ark., Jan'y 5, 1864, while another roll reports him as enlisted by Capt. Baxter, Nov'r 1st, 1863.

On this latter roll, also, the name of W. F. Younger is borne as 2d lieut. from Feb'y 1st, 1864, while on the rolls filed by the adjutant-general of Arkansas he is carried as a corporal.

Under the rulings of the Treasury Department, fraud in a portion of a claim taints the whole (Digest, Judge Advocate-General, page 87, section 10); "the military branch of the government is justified in withholding payment of any claim to which attaches a suspicion of fraud, which would invalidate such claim in law."

This in connection with the fact that contradictions as to when, where, and by whom many of the force were enlisted, clearly indicate an attempt to defraud the government, for which reason it is considered necessary to detail an officer, thereby incurring expense to the government, to proceed to Arkansas to investigate the minutia and merits of the claim, while the facts heretofore enumerated are deemed sufficient to predicate an adverse decision on the same.

It is therefore recommended that the rolls submitted be not accepted as satisfactory evidence, and that the claim be denied.

E. D. TOWNSEND,
Adjutant-General.

The Secretary of War declines to accept the rolls in question as evidence of service. Senator Clayton informed in person by the Sec'y of War. The Hon. E. Baxter to be informed by letter; reasons to be stated.

(Across the face:) Thomas M. Vincent,
Ass't Adj't General.
(Across the face:) See letter June 28, '72, to Hon. E. Baxter."

WASHINGTON, D. C., *June 12th*, 1872.

To the SECRETARY OF WAR:

SIR: Under an order from Maj. Gen'l F. Steele, commanding the army of Arks., dated October the 23rd, 1863, I recruited and enlisted a reg't of loyal Arkansans in the vicinity of Batesville, known as the 4th Arks. Mounted Infantry Vol's, and commanded the same as provisional colonel until the 12th day of May, 1864, when, in consequence of my election to a civil position, the command devolved upon Capt. T. A. Baxter, until the 2nd of June, 1864, at which time the organization was disbanded by order of Maj. Gen'l Steele in consequence of the refusal of the War Department to receive the reg't as twelve-months men.

The original orders are in my possession, and copies are on file in the War Department. The first company of this command was partially organized within ten days from the date of the original order, and from that time forward until they were disbanded the officers and men of the reg't performed regularly all the duties devolving upon them as soldiers under the orders of their superior officers, and orders from headquarters dist. N. E. Arkans., drawing arms, quartermaster and commissary stores as other troops. Several men were killed in battle, and others wounded and taken prisoners by the enemy.

This reg't was not mustered for the want of an officer in the Dist. of N. E. Arkansas duly authorized to muster them.

A more extended historical account of the reg't, sworn to by myself and several other officers of the command, is on file in your department.

A joint resolution of Congress of March the 18th, 1870, provides for the payment of the officers and men of this command (I believe) upon the single condition that the Secretary of War shall be satisfied that service was actually performed by the reg't.

The Assistant Adjutant-General informed me that he had, after examination, recommended the rejection of the claim, but declined to give the grounds upon which the recommendation was made. The company rolls of the reg't were made out from reliable data, and is believed to be correct.

The men are loyal, and wish to be recognized.

Hoping that you may find it consistent with your duties as a public officer to order these claims paid,

I am, very truly, your ob't serv't,

ELISHA BAXTER.

My address is Batesville, Arks.

WAR DEPARTMENT, A. G. O.,
June 28, 1872.

Hon. ELISHA BAXTER,
Batesville, Arkansas:

SIR: Referring to your letter of the 12th inst. to the Secretary of War, and an interview of this date between him & Senator Clayton as to the payment of the claims of the members of the 4th Arkansas Mounted Infantry, I have resp'y to inform you that the Secretary of War has declined to accept the rolls submitted as satisfactory evidence of service, for the following reasons:

1. The returns of the district of Northeast Arkansas made at the time of the actual enlistment of the force & based on presence and regimental returns, show for the months of January, February, March, April, and May, 1864, a much smaller force in officers & men than that on and covered by the rolls submitted by the attorneys for the claimants.

Some men whose names appear on the rolls submitted have heretofore been paid as members of other organizations.

3. Notations setting forth the loss of horses, &c., appear on these rolls which are not enumerated on rolls heretofore filed in this office.

4. Men enlisted by one officer are claimed to have been enlisted by another, and even then the dates of enlistment are entirely at variance.

The attorney's rolls bear the name of a man as an officer, while on the rolls heretofore filed he is borne as a corporal.

5. The rolls as submitted certify to company organization existing, when 'tis known from the records of this office that the companies as such were never organized.

6. The foregoing in connection with the fact that contradictions as to when, where, & by whom many of the force were enlisted clearly indicates an attempt to defraud the government, and under the rulings of the Treasury Dep't fraud in a portion of a claim taints the whole, and justifies the military branch of the govt' in withholding payment of any claim to which attaches a suspicion of fraud, & which would invalidate such claim in law.

E. D. TOWNSEND,
Adjutant-General.

The following communication was sent to the Commissioner of Pensions in reply to the usual call for statement of service:

War Department, Adjutant-General's Office,
May 6, 1875.

Commissioner of Pensions:

All claims of members of the 4th Arkansas M't'd Infantry have been suspended by the War Department until the claimants shall have presented satisfactory evidence of actual service rendered.

The rolls heretofore submitted have not been accepted, and it is respectfully suggested that action on pension applications, by the Commissioner, be likewise suspended until the question of organization involved shall have been decided by this office.

THOMAS M. VINCENT,
Ass't Adj't-General.

United States Senate Chamber,
Washington, April 3, 1876.

The honorable the Secretary of War:

Dear Sir: I inclose petition of Capt. Wm. J. Patton, asking appropriations for certain soldiers therein referred to.

Please examine same and advise me fully as to all the facts and information touching the same, shown by the records of your department. Has any other application ever been made to any of the dept's for the relief herein asked? If so, what action was taken?

Please return petition in the answer.

Yours truly,

F. M. COCKRELL,
For Mil. Com'tee in U. S. Senate.

War Department,
Washington City, April 17, 1876.

Sir: Acknowledging the receipt of your reference of the petition of William J. Patton for payment of members of the four companies of the 4th Arkansas Cavalry, enlisted under an authority from Major-General Fred. Steele, I have the honor to inclose herewith a copy of the report of the Adjutant-General, which embraces information touching the several questions contained in your letter of the 3d instant.

I also return the petition of Mr. Patton.

Very respectfully, your obedient servant,

ALPHONSO TAFT,
Secretary of War.

Hon. F. M. Cockrell,
Of Committee on Military Affairs, United States Senate.

War Department, Adjutant-Gen'l's Office,
April 12, 1876.

Respectfully returned to the Secretary of War.

By act of Congress, approved March 18, 1870, the Secretary of War, upon the possession of evidence which, to him, might seem satisfactory, was directed to investigate the claims of the force known as the 4th Arkansas Mounted Infantry, enlisted for 12 months (without the sanction of the War Department) under an authority from Major-General Fred. Steele; and, if he found that the force performed actual service in full co-operation with and subject to the orders of the United States authorities, to cause the officers and enlisted men thereof to be paid the same rates as was allowed by law to other volunteer forces in the military service at the same time.

On the promulgation of this law numerous claims were presented, including sets of rolls, by claim agents and others.

Those claims were carefully investigated in connection with the official records of this office, and it was found:

1. That the returns of the district of N. E. Arkansas, made at the time of the actual enlistment of the force and based on presence, regimental, and post returns, show, for the months of Jan'y, Feb'y, March, April, and May, 1864, a much smaller force than that on and covered by the rolls submitted.

2. Men, whose names appear on the rolls referred to, have heretofore been paid as members of other organizations for the period for which pay is claimed.

3. Notations setting forth the loss of horses appear on one set of rolls, which are not enumerated on other rolls on file.

4. Men enlisted by one officer are claimed to have been enlisted by another, and even then the dates of enlistment, as claimed to have been made by each, are entirely at variance.

5. One set of rolls bears the name of a man as an officer, while on another he is borne as a corporal.

6. The rolls certify to company organizations existing, when it is known from the records of this office that the companies, as such, were never organized.

The foregoing, in connection with the fact that contradictions as to when, where, and by whom many of the force were enlisted, indicated clearly that fraud permeated the claims to a greater or less extent, and, under the rulings of the Treasury Department, that fraud in a portion of a claim invalidated the whole and justified the military branch of the government in withholding any claim to which was attached a suspicion of fraud, which would invalidate such claim in law, the department declines to accept the rolls submitted as correct evidence of service.

The foregoing facts were officially communicated to Hon. Elisha Baxter, June 28, 1872, and to his attorneys, Messrs. Lowe and Archer, on May 13, 1875.

Since the latter date no new evidence has been submitted in the premises.

The bill for the relief of the 4th Arkansas M't'd Infantry was carefully prepared by the War Department, alike to protect the interests of the government as well as those of all legal claimants, and it is held that, as the law now stands, any and all just claims can be met without further legislation by Congress.

The petition of Mr. Wm. J. Patton is returned herewith.

E. D. TOWNSEND,
Adjutant-General.

HOUSE OF REPRESENTATIVES,
Washington, D. C., Dec. 19th, 1876.

Hon. J. D. CAMERON,
Secretary of War:

SIR: Inclosed I have the honor to hand you bill & joint resolution relating to the service of the 4th Arkansas Mounted Infantry Vols. I will be much obliged for any information in War Dep't bearing upon the merits of the claims set forth in said bill & resolution.

Very respectfully,

J. M. GLOVER,
Ch. Subcommittee on Military Affairs.

P. S.—Please return the bill & the joint resolution.

J. M. G., *Ch.*

The Secretary of War has the honor to return to the House of Representatives, for the Committee on Military Affairs, the bill and joint resolution (H. R. 121, 41st Congress, 2d session, and H. R. 1264, 44th Congress, 1st session) relating to the service of the 4th Arkansas Mounted Infantry Volunteers, and in compliance with the request of honorable J. M. Glover, of said committee, for any information bearing upon the merits of the claims, to enclose a report of the Adjutant-General upon the subject, dated the 4th instant.

J. D. CAMERON,
Secretary of War.

WAR DEPARTMENT.

WAR DEPARTMENT, ADJ'T GEN'L'S OFFICE,
January 4, 1877.

To the Hon. SECRETARY OF WAR:

SIR : In reply to your reference of H. R. No. 1264, "explaining and amending the provisions of a joint resolution passed by Congress March 18, 1870, for the benefit of the 4th Arkansas M't'd Infantry Vols.," I have the honor to report that Maj. Gen. F. Steele, U. S. Vols., authorized, Oct. 23d, 1863, the 4th Ark. M't'd Inf't'y, to be recruited for 12 months' service. There was no law for such an authorization, and it was given without the knowledge or sanction of the War Dep't.

By telegram from the superintendent of the volunteer recruiting service for Arkansas, dated April 20, 1864, it was reported that upwards of 300 men, enlisted for 12 months, were at Batesville, Arkansas, and that the intended colonel (Elisha Baxter) who had been authorized by Gen'l Steele to recruit the reg't, gave assurance that the members of the force would enlist for 3 years, if their muster could be dated back to time of original enlistment, so that they could receive the benefits arising from such muster. This was the first notice the Dep't had of the organization.

Upon the matter being submitted to the Secretary of War he decided that "the 300 men at Batesville may be enlisted for 3 years, and musters dated back to cover 12 months term. In so doing, no right or claim will be granted for any other bounty than the $100 (dollars) provided by act of 1861," and that decision was communicated by telegram, dated April 27, 1864.

It appears that the men did not accept the conditions and did not enlist as authorized by the Secretary of War.

It seems, however, that they rendered some service in good faith, as attested by Gen'l Steele's department returns, bearing as follows :

For January, 1864, 5 com'd off's and 222 enlisted men.

" February, 1864, 1*	"	"	270	"	"	
" March, 1864, 1	"	"	331	"	"	
" Ap'l, " 1	"	"	383	"	"	
" May, " 1	"	"	393	"	"	

After May, the force, which was never formally organized into companies, ceased to be accounted for, it having been disbanded June 2, 1864, by Special Orders 121, par. 2, from H'dq'rs Dep't of Arkansas.

With the view to prevent complications & difficulty in the adjustment of the claims of this force the original draft of the bill passed March 18, 1870, was submitted to this office Jan'y, 1870, by Hon. Mr. Slocum, M. C., then a member of the House Com. on Mil'y Affairs, and by it was altered & prepared so as to carefully guard alike the interests of the U. S. as well as those of all legal claimants. A copy of a report made at the time is herewith marked "A." †

The bill was passed in its amended form, and as contemplated by said report, with the exception of the following : Provided, That no payment shall be made for any time after the date the enlisted men declined to enlist for three years with a muster dated back to cover the 12 months term, as tendered by the War Dep't, by telegram through the Provost-Marshal-General, dated April 27, 1864.

The obstacles which have thus far precluded payments, under the bill, are, that immediately following its passage numerous claims & sets of rolls, purporting to be genuine, were presented by claim agents & others with view to payment, but which on close scrutiny were found to be unsatisfactory alike as to names, dates of enlistment, loss of horses & horse equipments, contrarieties as to rank, &c., while no two sets of rolls were alike. Under Sec. II of the proposed bill it would appear that it is the intention to recognize for pay the colonel & other officers of this force, the former of whom was merely a recruiting officer for it, & the others merely appointees of such recruiting officer, while there is no evidence that Recruiting Officer Baxter rendered a single day's field service. Should the proposed bill pass, so far as the "colonel & other officers" are concerned, it would be a precedent for the presentation of thousands of like claims to Congress, by persons engaged in recruiting co's & reg'ts, but who failed to complete them, thereby failing under the laws to secure either recognition or pay for contingent services in their capacities as private citizens.

As regards that portion of the same section of the bill which relates to the acceptance of the rolls, certified to by the gov. of the State of Arkansas, I have to state that there are none so certified on the files in this office.

In April, 1871, the then firm of Chipman, Hosmer & Co. filed 3 rolls, one of which was certified to by the Adj't Gen'l of Ark., one which that officer certified to as "unofficial," and one which was not certified to.

In October, 1871, the same firm presented 3 additional rolls, two of which were certified to by the A. G. of the State & one (a T. & S. roll) which was not.

On January 12, 1872, the Adj't Gen'l of Ark. forwarded 5 rolls, two of which are certified to, while the other 3 rolls are officially reported by him to be "unofficial."

* 4 com'd off's having been dropped as they were merely appointees of Recruiting Officer Baxter.
† See page 6, *ante*.

It will thus be seen that while Chip., Hos. & Co. have filed 6 sets of rolls, three of which are certified to, the Adj't Gen'l of the State in his communication to this office, certified to but two rolls. Also, that if the proposed bill should be passed in its present shape, aside from the numerous claims to which such action would give rise to, only two rolls could be accepted embracing an aggregate list of names of 161 officers and men in May, 1864, while the official records show an aggregate of one officer & 394 men under orders on that date. No rolls were filed in this office prior to 1870.

It is therefore submitted that as the law now stands all just claims can be met without further legislation by Congress, and to change the law would simply be in the interest of agents & attorneys & not further the interest of the enlisted men.

When this office shall have been reliably advised of the names of the enlisted men who were reported at Batesville, Ark., and the names of any who subsequently enlisted thus going to make the number on Gen'l Steele's Dep't Returns, with the dates as to service, &c., all necessary action by the War Dep't can be completed. The trouble thus far has been that would be officers, attorneys, & agents have been looking after money to the exclusion of the interests of the enlisted men, and in so doing have become connected with fraudulent attempts. It is proper to add that since the passage of the act of March 18, 1870, repeated efforts been made by this office through correspondence with Mr. Baxter and others to arrive at the facts, but thus far they have proved ineffectual.

I have the honor, &c.,

E. D. TOWNSEND,
Adj't General.

COMMITTEE ON MILITARY AFFAIRS,
HOUSE OF REPRESENTATIVES,
Washington, D. C., June 10th, 1878.

Hon. GEO. W. McCRARY,
Secretary of War:

SIR: I have the honor to request from you a duplicate of a report made by the War Department, in connection with S. 573, "for the relief of the officers and privates of the 4th Arkansas Cavalry Vols.," and which was filed with the papers of the case, when in the Senate, but which now appears to be lost.

I am, very respectfully,

ALVAH A. CLARK.

WAR DEPARTMENT,
Washington City, June 13th, 1878.

SIR: In response to your letter, dated the 10th instant, requesting a copy of a report of this department on S. 573, "for the relief of the officers and privates of the 4th Arkansas Cavalry Volunteers," I have the honor to transmit the copy* as requested.

Very respectfully, your obedient servant,

H. T. CROSBY,
Chief Clerk, for and in the absence of the Secretary of War.

Hon. ALVAH A. CLARK.
House of Representatives.

[Law office of Charles & George A. King, No. 916 F street, successors to Sanborn & King.]

WASHINGTON, D. C., *May* 17, 1882.

Hon. SECRETARY OF WAR:

SIR: On the 8th of February we had the honor to address the Adjutant-General, U. S. A., inclosing letters of the Hon. 2nd Auditor of the Treasury, relating to the claims of Solomon K. and Benjamin F. Chandler, for pay and bounty as late sergeant and private of Company A, 4th Regiment Arkansas Mounted Infantry Volunteers. The letters of the Hon. 2d Auditor stated that no action could be taken upon the claims referred to until the rolls of the said company had been perfected in the office of the Adjutant-General, and we requested to be informed as to what action had been taken under joint resolution of March 18, 1870 (16 Stat. at Large, 662). This act directs the Secretary of War to cause to be investigated the claims of the forces known as the 4th Arkansas Mounted Infantry, and if he finds the troops performed actual service, to cause the officers and soldiers thereof to be paid.

No answer was received to our inquiry, and on the 17th of March, 1882, we had the honor to ask attention to our previous letter to the Adjutant-General, and upon the 17th ult. we again wrote to the Adjutant-General, requesting an answer to the same

---

* See page 23, *ante.*

letter. At the present date we are not in receipt of any reply, and would therefore ask that we may be furnished at an early date with the desired information, if consistent with the rules of your department.

Very respectfully, your obedient servants,

CHARLES & GEORGE A. KING,
By WM. B. KING.

WAR DEPARTMENT, ADJUTANT-GENERAL'S OFFICE,
Washington, July 13, 1882.

To the honorable the SECRETARY OF WAR:

SIR: I have the honor to return herewith letter of Messrs. Charles and George A. King, attorneys, requesting information relative to the claims for pay and bounty of Solomon K. and Benjamin F. Chandler, late sergeant and private, respectively, of Company A, 4th Arkansas Mounted Infantry, and to invite attention to the inclosed copy of a report from this office, dated January 4, 1877,* which fully sets forth the status of the organization in question.

It is proper to add that under the provisions of the joint resolution, approved March 18, 1870, for the payment of the 4th Arkansas Mounted Infantry, the Secretary of War has made it a preliminary condition to the payment of this force, that duly authenticated rolls of the same shall first be accepted by the War Department and placed upon its files, but to this date such rolls have not been accepted, and until the terms of said condition shall have been complied with, this office will be unable to furnish any authentic information in regard to claims of members of this regiment.

It will also be seen from the report from this office of January 4, 1877, that it was impracticable to furnish satisfactory rolls of this organization immediately after the passage of the resolution, and such being the case, it is not believed to be practicable at this late date,

I am, sir, very respectfully, your obedient servant,

R. C. DRUM,
Adjutant-General.

WAR DEPARTMENT, *July 28, 1882.*

Respectfully returned to the Adjutant-General for report as to whether or not it is possible at this date to comply with part of the law touching the 4th Arkansas Mounted Infantry, as contained in the joint resolution of Congress approved March 18, 1870—16th Statutes at Large, page 662.

By order of the Secretary of War:

JOHN TWEEDALE,
Chief Clerk.

WAR DEPARTMENT, ADJUTANT-GENERAL'S OFFICE,
Washington, August 17, 1882.

To the honorable the SECRETARY OF WAR:

SIR: I have the honor to return herewith letter of Messrs. Charles and George A. King, attorneys, requesting information relative to the claims for pay and bounty of Solomon K. and Benjamin F. Chandler, late sergeant and private, respectively, of Company A, 4th Arkansas Mounted Infantry, returned to this office by you, the 28th ultimo, for report as to whether or not it is possible, at this date, to comply with part of the law touching the 4th Arkansas Mounted Infantry, as contained in the joint resolution of Congress, approved March 18, 1870, and to report thereon as follows:

Immediately after the passage of joint resolution referred to, various rolls of this force were presented by claim agents and others, which, upon investigation, were found to be so contradictory as to clearly indicate an attempt to defraud the government; and, subsequently, every effort was made by this office to secure proper rolls of the force, through Honorable E. Baxter, late acting colonel, Honorable Logan Root, M. C., and the State authorities, who were fully advised as to the data deemed necessary to establish the service of the members. To this date the data required has not been furnished, and, if it were so difficult a matter in 1870–1 to furnish satisfactory rolls, how much more difficult it will be after a lapse of twelve years, when some of the claimants and witnesses are deceased and the memories of those living have become impaired.

A compliance with the law, for the reasons stated, is, at this date, believed to be impracticable.

I am, sir, very respectfully, your obedient servant,

R. C. DRUM,
Adjutant-General.

---

* See page 23, *ante.*

WAR DEPARTMENT,
Washington City, August 22, 1882.

GENTLEMEN: The department is in receipt of your letter of May 17th last, inviting attention to your several communications addressed to the Adjutant-General, dated respectively February 8, March 17, and April 17, 1882, in regard to the claims of Solomon K. and Benjamin F. Chandler, for pay and bounty as late members of Company A, 4th Regiment of Arkansas Mounted Infantry Volunteers, and also inviting attention to certain letters from the Second Auditor of the Treasury, stating that no action could be taken upon the claims referred to until the rolls of said Company A had been perfected in the office of Adjutant-General.

In reply to your inquiry as to what action has been taken by the department under the joint resolution of Congress approved March 18, 1870 (16 Statutes, p. 662), I beg to enclose herewith a copy of a report, dated the 17th instant, from the Adjutant-General, from which it will be seen that all efforts heretofore made with the view of completing the rolls of said organization have proved unavailing, and that compliance with the law at this late date is deemed impracticable for the reasons set forth in said report.

Very respectfully,

ROBERT T. LINCOLN,
Secretary of War.

Messrs. CHARLES and GEORGE A. KING,
No. 916 F street, Washington, D. C.

A.—*Muster-roll of Captain James E. Conner, Company (C), of the Fourth Regiment of Arkansas Mounted Infantry Vols., United States Army, Colonel Elisha Baxter, from the first day of November, 1863, when last mustered, to the third day of June, 1864.*

No.	Names, present and absent.	Rank.	Joined for service and enrolled at general rendezvous; commencement of first payment by time.			Period.	Remarks.
			When.	Where.	By whom.		
	James E. Conner	Captain...	Nov. 1,1863	Jacksonport, Ark...	E. Baxter	1 year.	Elected 2d lieut. Nov. 1, 1863. Elected captain December 28th, 1863, vice Berry resigned.
	William P. Berry	Captain.	Dec. 28,'63	do. do.		do	Elected captain Nov. 1, 1863, and served until December 28th, 1863.
	John R. Wallard	1st lieut.	Jan. 7,1864	Batesville, Ark	Jas. E. Conner	do	" 1st lieut. Dec. 28th, 1863.
	James Palmer	2d lieut.	Nov. 1,1863	Jacksonport, Ark.	Elisha Baxter	do	Elected 2d lieut. Jan'y 7th, 1864.
1	Harrison W. Ball	1st sergt.	Nov. 1,'63	do.	do	do	
2	David B. Evans	Sergt	Nov. 1,'63	do	do	do	
3	James W. Brewer	do	Nov. 1,'63	do	do	do	
4	Benjamin F. Jackson	do	Nov. 1,'63	do	do	do	
5	William H. Cochrane	do	Nov. 1,'63	do	do	do	
6	Warren G. Ball	do	Nov. 1,'63	do	do	do	
7	Lewis R. Turner	do	Nov. 1,'63	do	do	do	
1	William H. Baker	Corporal	Nov. 1,'63	do	do	do	
2	O. B. Mobley	do	Nov. 1,'63	do	do	do	
3	James R. Maxley	do	Nov. 1,'63	do	do	do	
4	Absolem W Bullington	do	Nov. 1,'63	do	do	do	Lost horse & equipments in fight at Stoney Point, White Co., Ark., Nov. 25, 1863; also lost horse near Batesville, Ark., about 16th day of May, 1864.
5	Clinton M. Ball	do	Nov. 1,'63	do	do	do	
6	Francis M. King	do	Nov. 1,'63	do	do	do	
7	James W. Wallard	do	Nov. 1,'63	do	do	do	
1	Brawley, Hugh P.	Co. clk.	Nov. 1,'63	do	do	do	Lost horse and equipment in fight at Stoney Point, White Co., Ark., Nov. 25th, 1863.
2	Ball, Eldridge M.	Private	Nov. 1,'63	do	do	do	Captured and hung by the enemy about 5th of May, 1864.
3	Ball, George W	do	Nov. 1,'63	do	do	do	Lost horse and equipment near —— about —— May, 1864.
4	Barnwell, George W	do	Nov. 1,'63	do	do	do	Lost horse and equipments at fight at Stoney Point, Ark., Nov. 25, 1863; also lost horse at Waugh's, Jan. —, 1864.
5	Bassett, Franklin	do	Nov. 1,'63	do	do	do	
6	Bishop, William C	do	Nov. 1,'63	do	do	do	
7	Burrow, Ruzo	do	Nov. 1,'63	do	do	do	
8	Brown, John C	do	Nov. 1,'63	do	do	do	
9	Burris, John	do	Nov. 1,'63	do	do	do	Wounded and lost his horse and equipments at Stoney Point, White Co., Ark., Nov. 25, 1863.
10	Brewer, George W	do	Nov. 1,'63	do	do	do	
11	Brewer, Claiborne W	do	Nov. 1,'63	do	do	do	
12	Bone, E. J. K	do	Nov. 1,'63	do	do	do	Deserted May 28, 1864.
13	Conner, Isaac	do	Nov. 1,'63	do	do	do	
14	Cunningham, W. F	do	Nov. 1,'63	do	do	do	
15	Crisp, John	do	Nov. 1,'63	do	do	do	

A.—Master-roll of Captain Conner, Company (C), of the Fourth Regiment of Arkansas Mounted Infantry Vols., United States Army, &c.—Continued.

No.	Names, present and absent.	Rank.	Joined for service and enrolled at general rendezvous, commencement of first payment by time.				Remarks.
			When.	Where.	By whom.	Period.	
16	Crigler, William	Private	Nov. 1, '63	Jacksonport, Ark.	Elisha Baxter	1 year	Wounded in the shoulder in fight at Stoney Point, White Co., Ark., Nov. 25, 1863.
17	Dawson, Thomas J.	do	Nov. 1, '63	do	do	do	Died at Batesville, Ark., about Feb. 1st, 1864, in camp.
18	Fortinberry, Benjamin	do	Nov. 1, '63	do	do	do	
19	Fort, Aam H.	do	Nov. 1, '63	do	do	do	Lost horse and equipment at Stoney Point, White Co., Ark., Nov. 25th, 1863.
20	Gude, Benjamin F.	do	Nov. 1, '63	do	do	do	
21	Green, James M	do	Nov. 1, '63	do	do	do	
22	Gilliam, Harris	do	Nov. 1, '63	do	do	do	
23	Garner, Samuel	do	Nov. 1, '63	do	do	do	
24	Healey, M. N.	do	Nov. 1, '63	do	do	do	
25	Hardin, Madison	do	Nov. 1, '63	do	do	do	Killed in a skirmish in White Co., Ark., Nov. 25th, 1863.
26	Howe, Albert	do	Nov. 1, '63	do	do	do	
27	Harris, W. D.	do	Nov. 1, '63	do	do	do	
28	Haddock, Uriah	do	Nov. 1, '63	do	do	do	
29	Haddock, Calvin	do	Nov. 1, '63	do	do	do	
30	Hostetter, A	do	Nov. 1, '63	do	do	do	Killed by enemy about —— of ——, 1864.
31	Harvey, Benjamin A	do	Nov. 1, '63	do	do	do	
32	Harald, Madison B	do	Jan. 13, '64	Batesville, Ark.	Jno. R. Wallard	do	
33	Jackson, James S	do	Nov. 1, '63	Jacksonport, Ark.	E. Baxter	do	
34	King, Crockett	do	Nov. 1, '63	do	do	do	
35	King, W. H	do	Nov. 1, '63	do	do	do	
36	King, Henry C	do	Nov. 1, '63	do	do	do	
37	King, Henry A	do	Nov. 1, '63	do	do	do	
38	Lewallen, Monroe W	do	Jan. 5, '64	Batesville, Ark.	Jas. E. Conner	do	
39	Leggett, Albert	do	Nov. 1, '63	Jacksonport, Ark.	E. Baxter	do	
40	Lamons, James M	do	Nov. 1, '63	do	do	do	
41	Lawrence, Joseph	do	Nov. 1, '63	do	do	do	
42	Laboss, John	do	Apl. 19, '64	Batesville, Ark.	Jas. E. Conner	do	Killed by enemy.
43	Means, Samuel A	do	Nov. 1, '63	Jacksonport, Ark.	E. Baxter	do	
44	Marrow, William	do	Nov. 1, '63	do	do	do	
45	Nichols, John	do	Nov. 1, '63	do	do	do	
46	Nichols, Samuel J	do	Nov. 1, '63	do	do	do	
47	Perkins, James	do	Nov. 1, '63	do	do	do	Killed in Jackson County, Ark., about April 1st, 1864, while on scout.
48	Perkins, Solomon	do	Nov. 1, '63	do	do	do	
49	Palmer, John J	do	Nov. 1, '63	do	do	do	
50	Palston, John N	do	Nov. 1, '63	do	do	do	
51	Quimley, Richard B	do	Nov. 1, '63	do	do	do	
52	Reynolds, Robert	do	Nov. 1, '63	do	do	do	
53	Rogers, Elijah	do	Nov. 1, '63	do	do	do	Acted as regimental wagon-master from Feb. 1st, 1864.

No.	Name		Date	Place	By whom	Term	Remarks
54	Ross, Joseph	do	Nov. 1, '63	do	do	do	
55	Rust, John	do	Nov. 1, '63	do	do	do	
56	Rust, George W	do	Nov. 1, '63	do	do	do	
57	Sullivan, Holman	do	Nov. 1, '63	do	do	do	
58	Sullivan, Henry C	do	Nov. 1, '63	Jacksonport, Ark.	Elisha Baxter	1 yr.	Wounded in fight near Stoney Point, White Co., Ark., Nov. 25th, 1863.
59	Sergent, Charles C	do	Jan. 7, '64	Batesville, Ark.	Jas. E. Conner	do	
60	Scroggins, William A	do	Nov. 1, '63	Jacksonport, Ark	E. Baxter	do	
61	Scroggins, Ran.	do	Nov. 1, '63	do	do	do	
62	Simmons, Malcolm S	do	Nov. 1, '63	do	do	do	
63	Sinward, Hilbrom S	do	Nov. 1, '63	do	do	do	
64	Sinward, Joseph	do	Nov. 1, '63	do	do	do	
65	Sennard, James T	do	Nov. 1, '63	do	do	do	
66	Winston, John F	do	Nov. 1, '63	do	do	do	Lost horse and equipment in fight at Stoney Point, White Co., Ark., Nov. 25, 1863.
67	Williamson, Daniel	do	Nov. 1, '63	do	do	do	
68	Wren, Warren	do	Nov. 1, '63	do	do	do	
69	Wearns, Thomas	do	Nov. 1, '63	do	do	do	
70	Wood, James	do	Nov. 1, '63	do	do	do	
71	Walker, Absolem	do	Nov. 1, '63	do	do	do	
72	Wilson, James	do	Nov. 1, '63	do	do	do	
73	Young, John N	do	Nov. 1, '63	do	do	do	
74	Young, Henry H	do	Nov. 1, '63	do	do	do	
75	Yearkey, Henry C	do	Nov. 1, '63	do	do	do	
76	Yourbough, John	do	Nov. 1, '63	do	do	do	
77	Barnwell, Peter	do	Nov. 1, '63	do	do	do	Killed in fight with enemy near Stoney Point, White Co., Ark., about the 25th, 1863; also lost his horse and equipment at same time.
78	Dawson, Carroll	do	Nov. 1, '63	do	do	do	

Indorsed:) Muster-roll of Company C, of the 4th Regiment of Ark. Mounted Infantry Vols., from the 1st day of November, 1863, to the 3d day of June, 1864.

I certify, on honor, that this muster-roll is made out in the manner required by the *printed notes;* that it exhibits the true state of Captain James E. Conner Company (C) of the 4th Regiment of Ark. Mounted Inf'y Vols. for the period herein mentioned; that the "remarks" set opposite the name of each officer and soldier are accurate and just.

STATION: ——— ———.
DATE: June 21st, 1870.

JAMES E. CONNER,
Late Capt., Commanding the Company.

STATE OF ARKANSAS,
County of Independence, ss :

On this 21st day of June, 1870, personally appeared before me, a notary public in and for the county and State aforesaid, James E. Conner, of the county of Independence and State of Arkansas, who, being duly sworn according to law, declares that he is the identical person who was captain Company C, Fourth Arkansas Mounted Infantry Volunteers; that the accompanying muster-roll of said company, to which this affidavit is annexed, was made out under my direction; that I have carefully examined the same; that the list of said company is taken from a company book kept by me while in said company, and now in my possession; and that he believes said muster-roll to be correct; that said company, under the command of Capt. Wm. P. Berry, was received by Elisha Baxter, late provisional colonel of said Fourth Arkansas Mounted Infantry Volunteers, on or about the 24th day of October, 1863, but by mutual consent the enlistment was to date November 1, 1863; that when said company was received into the service by Elisha Baxter they were nearly all mounted, and that most of these men used their horse during almost the entire time they were in said company.

JAMES E. CONNER.

Sworn and subscribed to before me this 21st day of June, 1870.
[SEAL.]   WM. H. ROSE, *N. P.*

B.—*Muster-roll of the field and staff of the 4th Regiment of Ark. M't'd Inf. Volunteers, in the service of the United S'a'es, serving at Bate♥lle, Ark., under command of Colonel R. R. Livingston, of the First Reg't of Nebraska Cavalry Volunteers, from the 15th day of November, 1863, when last mustered, to the second day of June, 1861.*

Names, present and absent.	Rank.	Mustered into service.			Last paid.		Remarks.
		When.	Where.	By whom.	Period.	Served to what time.	
Elisha Baxter	Colonel	1863. Nov. 15th	Little Rock	Maj. Gen'l Steele	One year	Apr. 15, 1864	The field and staff (as well as the battalion) were on duty from November the 15th, 1863, date of entry into service, until June 2d, the date of discharge through orders received from H'dq'rs Dep't of Ark. They were never regularly mustered nor paid. The only commission issued to any of the command was the order issued by Maj. Gen'l Steele, com'd'g Dep't of Ark., authorizing Col. Elisha Baxter to organize the battalion.
Martin Reem	Adjutant	"	"	"	"	Apr. 15, 1864	
John J. Palmer	Q'rmaster	June 15, 1864	Batesville	Elisha Baxter	"	June 15, 1864	
William H. Ross	Adj't	Apr. 15, 1864	"	"	"	June 4, 1864	

The undersigned was only in command from the date of the order of General Steele authorizing the raising of the regiment until the early part of April, 1864.
Examined and approved.
Feb. 10th, A. D. 1871.

ELISHA BAXTER,
Late Provisional Col. 4th Ark's M. I. Vols.

(Indorsed:) A true copy of roll on file in the Adjutant-General's Dep't, State of Ark.
I certify, on honor, that this muster-roll is made out in the manner required by the printed notes; that it exhibits the true state f t he field and staff of the 4th Regiment of Ark. M't'd Inf. Vols, for the period herein mentioned; and that the "Remarks" set opposite the name of each officer and soldier are accurate and just.
STATION: Duvall's Bluff, Ark.
DATE: June 2d, 1864

Commanding the Regi...nt.

C.—*Muster-roll of Captain L. M. Harris, Company —, of the Fourth Regiment of Ark. Mounted Infantry Vol's, United States Army, Colonel Elisha Baxter, from the —— day of ——, 186-, to the —— day of ——, 186-.*

No.	Names, present and absent.	Rank.	When.	Where.	By whom.	Age.	Period.	Remarks.
			1864.	Batesville, Ark.	L. M. Harris		One year.	
1	L. M. Harris	Capt	Jan. 1, '64	Batesville, Ark.	L. M. Harris	40	One year.	
1	Brice M. Garner	1st serg't	"	"	"	24	"	
2	Wm. Ash	2d "	"	"	"	30	"	
3	David C. Bradford	3d "	"	"	"	22	"	
4	Henry Peters	4th "	"	"	"	38	"	
2	Allen, George W	Private	Mar. 15, '64	"	"	37	"	
3	Brown, Wm. H	"	" 1, '64	"	"	21	"	
4	Brantley, Benj. P	"	Jan'y 1 '64	"	"	44	"	
5	Brazeal, William	"	Mar. 15, '64	"	"	37	"	
6	Bonher, Andrew	"	" 20, '64	"	"	40	"	
7	Bochan, William	"	Jan., 1, '64	"	"	18	"	
8	Bishop, William	"	"	"	"	24	"	
9	Brown, George	"	"	"	"	26	"	
10	Cornwell, John R	"	Mar. 15, '64	"	"	41	"	
11	Chambers, Wm. R	"	Jan. 1, '64	"	"	24	"	
12	Cartright, John	"	Mar. 15, '64	"	"	30	"	
13	Compton, Thos. J	"	Jan. 1, '64	"	"	26	"	
14	Ducker, John L	"	Mar. 1, '64	"	"	40	"	
15	Daniels, William	"	"	"	"	29	"	
16	Zoff, Stephens	"	Jan. 1, '64	"	"	21	"	
17	Emmons, Griffin	"	" 20, '64	"	"	19	"	
18	Emmons, John W	"	Feb. 15, '64	"	"	17	"	
19	Elliott, Stephen	"	"	"	"	24	"	
20	Ellis, William	"	"	"	"	29	"	
21	Gadberry, William H	"	Jan. 1, '64	"	"	23	"	
22	Gibson, Lebanon J	"	Mar. 1, '64	"	"	24	"	
23	Gibson, William J	"	"	"	"	22	"	
24	Harp, William H	"	Feb. 15, '64	"	"	20	"	
25	Harp, John L	"	"	"	"	24	"	
26	Handricks, Jas. R. P	"	"	"	"	18	"	
27	Hendricks, Isaac R	"	"	"	"	33	"	
28	Hufstedler, Jacob	"	"	"	"	27	"	
29	Hubbell, L. B	"	Jan. 1, '64	"	"	35	"	
30	Huntley, Charles	"	"	"	"	24	"	
31	Hull, George	"	"	"	"	24	"	
32	Huson, George W	"	Mar. 1, '64	"	"	24	"	
33	Hammonds, James H	"	Jan. 1, '64	"	"	25	"	
34	Horten, Elijah	"	"	"	"	26	"	Died in hospital at Batesville, Ark., March 26th, 1864.

No.	Name								Date		
35	Holsenback, David C			24					Jan. 15, '64		
36	Hilton, Jessie W			16					Mar. 15, '64		
37	Hilton, James T			25							
38	Ivey, James			18					Mar. 30, '64		
39	Ivey, Greene			36							
40	Lindsey, James H			30					Mar. 1, '64		
41	Lancaster, Allen P			18					Mar. 15, '64		
42	Lancaster, James M			23					Jan. 1, '64		
43	Lancaster, Perrin W			23							
44	Lancaster, Charles			19					Mar. 15, '64		
45	Lindsay, Dixon M			20							
46	Laveaon, Archie			20					Jan. 1, '64		
47	Lemmons, Ancas J			24					Feb. 15, "		
48	Lemmons, John P			34					Jan. 1, "		
49	Michel, Geo. W			18							
50	Milligan, James			29					Jan. 15, '64		
51	McCorkle, Thomas			23					Mar. 1, "		
52	McCorkle, Samuel			22							
53	Melton, Thomas			27							
54	Noblin, Samuel J			36					Jan. 15, '64		
55	Noblin, Cullen			36					Feb. 15, '64		
56	Nicholas, Edmond			31					Mar. 22, "		
57	Nicholas, Joseph			24					Mar. 20, '64		
58	Puryear, James M			36							
59	Pollard, James H			44					Feb. 15, '64		
60	Prewitt, Lewis H			26					Jan. 1, "		
61	Parker, Milton J			26					Jan. 1, "		
62	Peters, John			27					Jan. 1, "		
63	Payne, Anderson H			25					Jan. 1, "		
64	Pritchard, Henry J			38					Mar. 1, "		
65	Pritchard, James H			21							
66	Philbrook, Samuel			29					Jan. 1, "		
67	Pyland, John E			27					Feb. 15, "		
68	Ried, Henry			37					Jan. 1, "		
69	Rone, James			18							
70	Russell, William M			35					Mar. 1, "		
71	Stafford, William H			30					Jan. 15, "		
72	Sanders, W. P			25							
73	Stamps, John			29							
74	Stark, Frank			30					Jan. 1, "		
75	Snoblin, Thomas			28					Feb. 15, "		
76	Stayton, Greene D			18							
77	Stayton, Wm. P			18							
78	Simons, Wm. S			25							
79	Treadway, Wm. H			31					Apl. 1, '04		
80	Teal, Andrew J			30					Mar. 15, "		
81	Terill, Wm. C			18					Feb. 15, "		
82	Vaughn, John M			18							
83	Warlick, James W			25					Feb. 1, '64		
84	Wilson, Edward H			31					Mar. 15, "		
85	Williams, Amasa M			22					Jan. 1, "		
86	Williams, Asa			19					Jan. 1, "		

C.—*Muster-roll of Captain L. M. Harris' Company (—), of the Fourth Regiment of Ark. Mounted Infantry Vol's, United States Army, Colonel Elisha Baxter, from the —— day of ——, 184-, when last mustered, to the —— day of ——, 186- .—Continued.*

No.	Names, present and absent.	Rank.	Joined for service and enrolled at general rendezvous; commencement of first payment by time.				Period.	Remarks.
			When.	Where.	By whom.	Age.		
87	Williams, Anderson A	Private	Jan. 1, '64	Batesville, Ark	L. M. Harris	22	One year	Killed in skirmish at Lewisburg, Ark., Jan. 22, 1864.
88	White, John	"	" 1, "	"	"	20	"	
89	Walker, George	"	" 1, "	"	"	24	"	

A true copy of unofficial rolls on file in the adjutant-general's office of Arkansas.

Examined and approved Feb. 10, A. D. 1871.

KEYES DANFORTH, *Adj't General.*

ELISHA BAXTER,
Late Provisional Colonel 4th Arkansas Mounted Infantry.

(Indorsed:) Muster-roll of Company E, of the 4th Regiment of Ark. M. Inf. Vols, from the —— day of ——, 186-, to the —— day of ——, 186- .

D.—*Muster-roll of Captain* ———, *Company (B), of the* ——— *Regiment of* ———, *United States Army, Colonel* ———, *from the* ——— *day of* ———, 186—, *when last mustered, to the* —— *day of* ———, 186—.

Names, present and absent.	Rank.	Enlistment.	Remarks.
Geo. W. Robertson . ..	1st lieut .	....	Elected lieut. Jan'y 28th, 1864.
Solomon K. Chandler....	1st serg't .	Dec. 1, 1863	Appointed 1st sergeant Jan'y 30th, 1864.
J. E. Jones	Serg't.....	" " "	" sergeant " "
G. H. Pinkston	Corporal..	" " "	Appointed corporal Jan'y 30th, 1864.
G. W. Goad	"	Jan. 27, 1864	" " Feb'y 10th, "
J. E. Gifford	"	" 30 "	" " " " "
Adams, B. F ...	Private ...	Dec. 1, 1863	
Anderson, Isaac........		Jan. 18, 1864	
Anderson, J. W ....,......		Dec. 15, 1863	Captured in skirmish at Holt's Mill, Ark., Feb'y
Bishop, Joseph........'........		Jan. 18, 1864	10, 1864; clothing, horse, and equipments taken
Bishop, W. A..... ...'.........		" 22, 1864	from him.
Bryson, R. J............		Dec. 1, 1863	
Barrber, A. A		Mar. 22, 1864	
Chandler, B. F............		Dec. 1, 1863	
Cochran, Henry ...,.....		Jan. 15, 1863	
Carter, J. E.............		Jan. 27, 1864	
Dugger, A. M		Dec. 1, 1863	
Dolin, William ....|........		Mar. 29, 1864	
Embry, G. M		" 23 "	
Embry, W. M ....'.........			
Embry, D. C		" .. "	
Ford, R. F		Jan. 27, "	
Ford, W. R ....'.........		" " "	
Goad, J. J		" 15 "	Deserted May 30, 1864, at Jacksonport. Ark.
Gire, W. H		Dec. 1, 1863	
Hicks, G. C............		Mar. 17, ."	
Hamley, A. R. D		Feb. 1, 1864	
Hamley, A. N. M ......'........		" " "	
Huff, W. B		Dec. 15, 1863	
Hall, E. E		Jan. 25, 1864	
Hall, J. A		" " "	
Harris, Simeon		" 27 "	
Hunt, A. M		Mar. 14, "	
Hawkins, S. D		" 21 "	
Johnson, B. D		" 22 "	
Lane, Bird		Jan. 25, "	
Lingo, Moses		Mar. 9, "	
McGee, J. R. P		Dec. 15, 1863	
McCrary, F. E............		" 1 "	
McLeod, Mills............		Feb. 1, 1864	Captured and his clothing taken from him.
Morgan, J. D ....,........		Jan. 21, "	
Massey, Eli		" 14 "	
Mobley, Calvin		Feb. 18, "	
Montgomery, James		Apr. 12, "	
Norris, W. R		Jan. 25, "	Captured and his clothing taken from him.
Pinkston, Phineas............		Dec. 15, 1863	
Privett, Jesse		Jan. 18, 1864	
Price, J. G............		Mar. 14, "	
Price, L. C............		" " "	
Price, Wm ....,.........		Apr. 1, "	Deserted May 30, 1864, at Jacksonport Ark.
Rodgers, G. M. D		Dec. 1, "	
Rensick, Henry		Jan. 28, "	Lost horse and equipments in action Feb'y 10, 1864.
Suddith, Gerard............		Dec. 15, 1863	
Snick, G. W		Jan. 27. 1864	
Sarope, John ....'........		Dec. 15, 1863	
Scroggins, G. W ....|........		Mar. 14, 1864	
Simpson, A. A ....|........		Jan. 29. "	
Sellers, T. W		" 26 "	
Smith, J. E ....|.........		Feb. 5, "	
Smith, W. T............		" 18. "	
Stout, H. H .... |........		Mar. 22, "	Deserted May 30, 1864, at Jacksonport, Ark.
Stevens, G. W		Apr. 26, "	
Tindle, R. P		Jan. 18, "	
Wolf, John............		" 25, "	
Wilson, C. D ....|........		Dec. 15, 1863	
Wasson, J. B		Feb. 5, 1864	
Wilkerson, F. A............'.........			
Whitlaw, S. C ....|.........		Jan. 27, "	
Ward, Jasper		Apr. 14, "	Deserted May 30, 1864, at Jacksonport, Ark.
Wolf, David............|.........		Jan. 25, "	

A true copy of the rolls on file in the adjutant-general's office of Arkansas.

KEYES DANFORTH, *Adjutant-General.*

Examined and approved Feb'y 10, A. D., 1871.

ELISHA BAXTER,
Late Provisional Col. of the 4th Arkansas Mounted Infantry.

(Indorsed:) Muster-roll of Company B, of the 4th Regiment of Ark. M't'd Inf'y Vols., from the ——— day of ———, 186—, to the ——— day of ———, 186—.

F.—Muster-roll of Captain James E. Conner, Company (C), of the Fourth (4th) Regiment of Arkansas Mounted Infantry, United States Army, Colonel Elisha Baxter, from the 1st day of November, 1863, when enlisted into service, to the 3d day of June, 1864, when discharged.

No.	Names, present and absent.	Rank.	When.	Where.	By whom.	Period.	Remarks.
1	James E. Conner	Capt	Dec. 28, '63	Jacksonport, Ark	E. Baxter	One year	Elected 2d lt. Nov. 1, 1863, & capt. co. Dec. 28, 1863, vice Berry, resigned.
1	Wm. P. Berry	Capt					Elected capt. Nov. 1, 1863, and resigned Dec. 28, 1863.
1	John R. Wallard	1st lt	Dec. 28, '63	Batesville	Jas. E. Conner		" 1st lieut. Dec. 28, 1863.
2	James Palmer	2d lt	Jan'y 7, '64				" 2d lieut. Jan'y 7, 1864.
1	Harrison M. Ball	1st s'g't	Nov. 17, '63	Jacksonport	E. Baxter		
2	David Evans	S'g't					
3	James W. Brewer						
4	Benjamin F. Jackson						
5	William H. Cochrane						
6	Warren G. Ball						
7	Lewis R. Turner						Lost horse & equipment in engagement near Stony Point, Ark., Nov. 25, 1863.
1	William H. Baker	Corp'l					Lost horse & equipment in engagement near Stony Point, Ark., Nov. 25, 1863. Lost a horse near Batesville, Ark., in an engagement, May 15, 1864.
2	O. B. Mobley						
3	James R. Maxley						
4	Absolam W. Bullington						
5	Clinton M. Ball						
6	Francis M. King						
7	James M. Willard						
1	Brawley, Hugh P	Pv't					Lost horse & equipment in engagement near Stony Point, Ark., Nov. 25, 1863.
2	Ball, Eldridge M						Captured and hung by enemy, May 5, 1864.
3	Ball, George W						Lost horse and equipment, May, 1864.
4	Barnwell, George W						Lost horse & equipment in engagement near Stony Point, Ark., Nov. 25, 1863; also lost horse & equipment in engagement near Waugh's, Jan'y 10, 1864.
5	Bassett, Franklin						
6	Bishop, William C						
7	Burrow, Renzo						
8	Brown, John G						Wounded, and lost horse & equipment at Stony Point, Ark., Nov. 25, 1863.
9	Barris, John						
10	Brewer, George W						
11	Brewer, C. W						
12	Bone, E. J. K						Deserted May 28, 1864.
13	Conner, Isaac						

Joined for service and enrolled at general rendezvous; commencement of first payment by time.

No.	Name	Date	Place	By whom enlisted	Term	Remarks
14	Cunningham, Wm. F					
15	Crisp, John					
16	Crigler, William					Died at Batesville about Feb. 1, 1864.
17	Dawson, Thomas J					
18	Dawson, Carroll					
19	Fortenberry, Benjamin					
20	Fort, Adam M					Lost horse & equipment in engagement, Stony Point, Ark., Nov. 25, 1864.
21	Goode, Benjamin F					
22	Greene, James M					
23	Gillam, Harris					
24	Garner, Samuel					
25	Henley, M. N					
26	Howe, Albert					
27	Harris, W. D					
28	Haddock, Triah					
29	Haddock, Calvin					
30	Hosteller, A					
31	Harvey, Benjamin A	Jan'y 15, '64	Batesville	J. R. Wallard		
32	Harald, Madison B	Nov. 5, '63	Jacksonport	E. Baxter		
33	Jackson, James S					
34	King, Crockett H					
35	King, Wm. H					
36	King, Henry C					
37	King, Henry A					
38	Lewallen, Monroe W					
39	Leggett, A					
40	Lannons, James M					
41	Lawrence, Joseph					
42	LaJuas, John	Ap'l 19, '64	Batesville	Jas E. Conner		
43	Means, Samuel A	Nov. 1, '63	Jacksonport	E. Baxter		
44	Marrow, William					
45	Nichols, John					
46	Nichols, Samuel					
47	Perkins, James					Killed in Jackson County, Ark., Ap'l 1, 1864, on scout.
48	Perkins, Soloman					
49	Palmer, John, jr					
50	Polston, John N					
51	Quinby, Richard B					
52	Reynolds, Robert					Acted as regimental wagonmaster from April 1, 1864.
53	Rogers, Elijah					
54	Russ, Joseph					
55	Russ, John					
56	Rust, George W				One year	
57	Sullivan, Holman	Nov. 1, '63	Jacksonport	E. Baxter		
58	Sullivan, Henry C					
59	Sergent, Charles C					
60	Scroggins, William A					
61	Simmons, Malcolm S					
62	Sinnard, Wilburn S					
63	Sinnard, Joseph					
64	Sinnard, James T					

E.—*Muster-roll of Captain James E. Conner, Company (C), of the Fourth (4th) Regiment of Arkansas Mounted Infantry, &c.*—Continued.

No.	Names, present and absent.	Rank.	When.	Where.	By whom.	Period.	Remarks.
65	Scroggins, Ian	Pv't	Nov. 1, '63	Jacksonport	E. Baxter	One year	Wounded in engagement near Stony Point, Ark. Nov. 25, 1863.
66	Winston, John F						
67	Williamson, Daniel						
68	Wren, Warren						
69	Weaver, Thomas						
70	Wood, James						
71	Walker, Absalom						
72	Wilson, James						
73	Young, John N						
74	Young, Henry H						
75	Yearkey, Henry C						
76	Yearbrough, John						
	Barnwell, Peter						Killed in an engagement with the enemy near Stony Point. Ark. Nov. 25, 1863 ; also lost horse and equipment.
	Hardin, Madison J						Killed in an engagement with the enemy near Stony Point. Ark. Nov. 25, 1865.

Examined and approved the 10th of Feb., A. D. 1871.

JAMES E. CONNER,
Late Captain Co. C, 4th Reg't of Arkansas Mounted Infantry Vols.

ELISHA BAXTER,
Late Provisional Col., 4th Arkansas Mounted Infantry.

(Indorsed:) Muster-roll of Company C, of the 4th Regiment of Ark.- M't'd Inf. from the —— day of ——, 186—, to the —— day of ——, 186—.

STATE OF ARKANSAS, *County of Independence, ss :*

On this 10th day of February, 1871, personally appeared before me, a county clerk in and for the county and State aforesaid, James E. Conner, of the county of Independence, and State of Arkansas, who, being duly sworn according to law, deposes that he is the identical person named in the foregoing muster-roll of Company C, of the Fourth Regiment of Arkansas Moun ed Infantry Volunteers, as captain of said company, and that he has signed said roll as captain ; that said company roll he believes to be correct, as it has been made from a company book of said company kept by him while in said regiment, and which has been in his possession ever since ; that each and every man whose name appears upon said roll actually performed the service therein claimed for him ; that most of his company were mounted upon their own private horses during the time this company was in the United States service.

JAMES E. CONNER.

Subscribed & sworn to before me this 10th day of February, A. D. 1871.

[SEAL.]

REUBEN HAYSHAM, *Clerk.*

F.—*Muster-roll of Captain Moses Ford, Company (D), of the 4th Regiment of Mounted Inf. Vols. (Ark.), United States Army, Colonel Elisha Barter, from the 1st day of January, 1864, when last mustered, to the 2d day of June, 1864.*

No.	Names, present and absent.	Rank.	Joined for service and enrolled at general rendevous; commencement of first payment by time.				Remarks.
			When.	Where.	By whom.	Period.	
			1864.				
1	Moses Ford	Capt.	June 1	Batesville		One year	This company was discharged from the U. S. service at Du-Vall's Bluff, Ark., June 2, 1864, by order from Hd. Qrs. Dept. of Ark., June 2, 1864.
1	Wm. M. Younger	2d lt	Feb. 1	Batesville	Moses Ford	One year	Promoted to 2d lieutenant Feb. 1, 1864.
2	Robt. S. Sanders	1 sergt	Apr. 15	"	"		
3	Chas. W. White	Sergt	"	"			
	Carly Mosier	"	Jan. 1				
4	Robb Jn. Baker	"	" 15				
1	Wm. J. Daniels	Corporal		Batesville	Moses Ford	One year	
2	Henry A. Miller	"		"			Killed in action Feb. 15.
3	Martin Speaks	"	Apr. 15				
4	Wm. M. Younger	"	Jun. 1				Promoted to 2d lieutenant Feb. 1, 1864.
5	Wm. M. Ray	"					
6	Marcus P. Sipe	"	Feb. 1	Batesville	Moses Ford	One year	
1	Adrian, George W	Private	Apr. 20	"	"		
2	Atkinson, William	"	May 1				
3	Bandy, Williamson H	"	Mch. 15				
4	Blu, William J	"	Jan. 1				
5	Blu, Joseph	"					
6	Bryan, John H	"	15				
7	Bangs, Jacob	"					
8	Blagg, Samuel	"	Apr. 1				
9	Blake, Samuel T	"	Jan. 1				
10	Brown, Neal S	"	15				
11	Bramlet, John T	"					
12	Barksdale, John T	"	Apr. 1				
13	Brooks, James W	"					
14	Buckhart, John H	"	15				
15	Bundy, Ranson C	"	May 1				
16	Beckham, Rody	"					
17	Beckham, John	"					
18	Cuningham, Wm. P	"	Feb. 1				Died in hospital at Batesville, March 19, 1864.
19	Clark, Henry C	"	Jan. 1				
20	Coggeshall, James R	"					
21	Coggeshall, William	"					
22	Cole, Harrison	"	Mch. 15				
23	Canard, Joseph	"	15				
24	Dodds, Wm. J. C	"	Feb. 1				Dest.
25	Davis, James C. C	"					

F.—*Muster-roll of Captain Moses Ford, Company(D), of the 4th Regiment of Mounted Inf. Vols.(Ark.), United States Army, Colonel Elisha Baxter, &c.—Cont'd.*

No.	Names, present and absent.	Rank.	When.	Where.	By whom.	Period.	Remarks.
			1864.				
26	Davis, William	Private	Mch. 15	Batesville	Moses Ford	One year	
27	Dodd, Benjamin H	"	Apr. 15	"	"	"	
28	Fishback, Henry	"	Jan. 1	"	"	"	
29	Fishback, Charles	"	"	"	"	"	
30	Ferguson, George	"	Mch. 15	"	"	"	Dest.
31	Granger, Alexander	"	Jan. 1	"	"	"	
32	Gresso, James W	"	Jan. 15	"	"	"	
33	Godwin, Benjamin	"	"	"	"	"	
34	Grimes, David H	"	Feb. 1	"	"	"	
35	Greenway, James T	"	Apr. 15	"	"	"	
36	Harrison, Albert H	"	May 1	"	"	"	
37	Johnson, John L	"	Apr. 15	"	"	"	
38	Johnson, Elisha B	"	Jan. 15	"	"	"	
39	Johnson, William D	"	25	"	"	"	
40	Jones, James F	"	"	"	"	"	
41	Klinger, Charles	"	Apr. 15	"	"	"	
42	Killian, Joseph	"	Jan. 1	"	"	"	
43	Locke, William J	"	15	"	"	"	
44	Lively, Carter	"	Apr. 1	"	"	"	
45	Mosier, Burrell A	"	"	"	"	"	
46	Mills, James T	"	Jan. 1	"	"	"	
47	Mosier, John J	"	"	"	"	"	
48	McLaughlin, Mark B	"	Feb. 1	"	"	"	
49	Martin, Napoleon	"	"	"	"	"	
50	Mesir, John R	"	Mch. 15	"	"	"	
51	Mosier, Jacob	"	"	"	"	"	
52	Martin, Daniel	"	"	"	"	"	
53	Pumphrey, Franklin	"	Apr. 1	"	"	"	
54	Preston, Charles F	"	Jan. 1	"	"	"	Dest.
55	Painter, John W	"	"	"	"	"	Dest.
56	Pearce, Rayford F	Private	Jan. 28	Batesville	Moses Ford	One year	
57	Pittman, Matthew L	"	Apr. 1	"	"	"	
58	Pramposin, Victor	"	Jan. 15	"	"	"	
59	Russell, Christopher C	"	Jan. 1	"	"	"	
60	Ray, John T	"	"	"	"	"	
61	Roby, James	"	"	"	"	"	
62	Rollins, Charles	"	"	"	"	"	
63	Renner, David	"	"	"	"	"	
64	Sipes, William S	"	Apr. 15	"	"	"	
65	Sipes, Jacob P	"	Jan. 1	"	"	"	

No.	Name	Date
66	Sipes, Franklin	
67	Sipes, Rufus	
68	Smith, Enoch	
69	Smith, Leonidas	
70	Sanders, John F.	
71	Sommers, William	
72	Sullivan, Joseph D	Feb. 1
73	Smith, Leander	Mch. 1
74	Scroggins, Isaac	Apr. 15
75	Scott, Samuel	
76	Speak, Martin, Jr.	Jan. 1
77	Whiting, John W	Apr. 1
78	Whitfield, Reuben	
79	Wor, Esedore	" 15
80	Woodsell, George W	" 20
81	Young, Andrew J	Jan. 1
82	Young, William T	"

Examined and approved Feb. 10th, A. D. 1871.

(Indorsed:) Muster-roll of Company D of the 4th Regiment of Arkansas Mounted Infantry Volunteers, from the 1st day of Jan'y, 1864, to the 2d day of June, 1864.

NOTE.—These men were enlisted, and were immediately placed upon active duty, in which they continued until the date of their disbandment at Duvall's Bluff, Ark., Jan. 2d, 1864, by orders from Dept. Hd. Qrs., 7th Corps, Little Rock. They were never regularly mustered or paid, only sworn in and placed on duty.

I certify, on honor, that this muster-roll is made out in the manner required by the *printed notes*; that it exhibits the true state of Captain Moses Ford's Company (—) of the 4th (Fourth) Regiment of Ark. Mtd. Inf. Vols. for the period herein mentioned; that the "remarks" set opposite the name of each officer and soldier are accurate and just; and that the "recapitulation" exhibits in every particular the true state of the company, as required by Regulations and Rules and Articles of War.

Station: Duvall's Bluff, Ark.

Date: June 2d, 1864.

M. FORD, *Commanding the Company.*

A true copy of roll in the adjutant-gen'l's Dept., Arkansas.

STATE OF ARKANSAS,

KEYES DANFORTH, *Adjutant-General of Arkansas.*

ELISHA BAXTER,
Provisional Col. of the 4th Ark. Mounted Infantry.

County of Independence, *ss :*

On this 12th day of January, 1871, personally appeared before me, a county clerk in and for the county and State aforesaid, Moses Ford, of the county of Independence and State of Arkansas, who being duly sworn according to law declares and says that he is the identical person named upon the foregoing muster-roll as captain Company D of the Fourth Regiment of Arkansas Infantry Volunteers; that said roll is a copy of the roll on file in the office of the adjutant-general of Arkansas, and a correct copy of the roll retained by me, and now in my possession ; that said company performed actual service from the time its entering the United States service until the time of its discharge, on the 3d day of June, 1864, at Duvall's Bluff, Ark., in compliance with Special Order No. 121, from Headquarters Department of Arkansas, dated June 2, 1864.

MOSES FORD.

Sworn to before me this 12th day of January, 1871.

[SEAL.]

REUBEN HAYSHAM, *County Clerk.*

G.—*Muster-roll of Captain Taylor A. Baxter, Company (A), of the Fourth Regiment of Arkansas Mounted Infantry, United States Army, Colonel Elisha Baxter, from the —— day of ——, 186--, when last mustered, to the 3d day of June, 1864.*

Names, present and absent	Rank.	Enlistment.	Remarks.
T. A. Baxter	Capt	Jan. 1st, 1864	Commanding regt. since March 25th, 1864.
John W. Ayres	1st lieut	" " "	Commanding company since March 25th, 1864.
Noel G. Reaves	2d lieut	" " "	
Thos. W. Pyer	1st sergt	" " "	
John W. Carter	Sergt	" " "	
W. J. Roach	"	" " "	
C. J. Fuller	"	" " "	
M. J. Bradley	"	" " "	Wounded in skirmish February 19th, 1864.
W. A. Curtiss	Corporal	" " "	
A J Sherrill	"	17 "	
W. H. Fuller	"	Dec. 13, 1863	
J. C. Reynolds	"	Jan. 1st, 1864	
E. E. Rushing	"	" " "	
J. D. Massey	"	" " "	
J. M. Freeman	"	" " "	
Jas. H. Wyatt	"	" " "	
Allan. Marcus	Private	April 3d, 1864	
Arnold, Ralph	"	Jan. 1st, "	
Blevius. Alcana	"	Mar. 15th, "	
Berry, Spencer	"	Jan. 1st, "	
Bell, Wm. W	"	" " "	
Bass. Wm. M	"	" 4th, "	
Blevius, Oliver C	"	Feb. 5th, "	
Bryant. Wm. H	"	Jan. 29th, "	
Brown. Grisby	"	" 1st, "	Wounded in skirmish February 19th, 1864.
Burgess. Leroy	"	" " "	
Chastain, Alfred	"	April 6th, "	
Chastain. Joseph	"	" " "	
Chastain, Berry F	"	" " "	
Cravan, John M	"	Mar. 17th, "	
Chamoress, N. C	"	Jan. 13th, "	
Churchnell. Wm. P	"	" 1st, "	
Cooeston. A. J	"	Mar. 8th, "	
Curtis, John	"	Jan. 1st. "	
Curtis, Wm. R	"	" " "	
Davis. Elijah	"	" 8th. "	
Evans, David T	"	May 2d. "	
Evans. John T	"	" " "	
Fox. John O	"	Jan. 30th, "	
Foust, Ellison	"	" 1st, "	
Forrester. C. C	"	" 23d, "	
Forrester. Robt. C	"	" " "	
French. Wm	"	Mar. 26th. "	
Fuller. H. N	"	Jan. 1st. "	
Furgison, Ellis A	"	" 23d, "	
Holland, John G	"	" 1st, "	
Harris. Frank S	"	" " "	
Holt. Elijah	"	Feb'y 18th "	
Holt. Pleasant	"	" " "	
Hughes. F. M	"	Jan. 1st, "	
Hunt. W. J	"	" " "	
Hawk. S. M	"	" " "	
Knight, John	"	Feb'y 17th, "	
Knight. J. J	"	Mar. 5th, "	
Knight, M. V	"	Jan. 1st, "	
Knight, M. M	"	Mar. 5th, "	
Knight, L. T	"	Feb. 17th, "	
Knight, L. F	"	Apr. 8th, "	
Lacy, James	"	" 6th, "	
Liles, Wm. H. H	"	Jan. 12th, "	
Lemans, John R	"	Feb. 4th, "	
Lemans, Samuel	"	Mar. 15th, "	
Markham, Holland	"	Jan. 25th, "	
Mathis, Wm. J	"	" 14th, "	
Merritt, John C	"	" 1st, "	
McCyee, John C	"	" 19th, "	
Marshall, Wm	"	" 1st, "	
Meeks, Richard D	"	" 29th, "	
Nunn, Wm. P	"	Feb. 8th, "	
Nunnelly. Wm	"	Jan. 1st, "	
Owens, Thos. R	"	" " "	
Overstreet. James	"	" 30th, "	
Ozemont. Wm. L	"	" 1st. "	
Pool. Robt. N	"	" " "	
Pickel. Joseph	"	Mar. 15th "	
Reynolds. George M	Private	Jan. 1st. 1864	
Rhoades, Jackson	"	" " "	
Snodgrass, Geo. D	"	" " "	

G.—*Muster-roll of Captain Taylor A. Baxter, &c.—Continued.*

Names, present and absent.	Rank.	Enlistment.	Remarks.
Scruggs, W. R. N	Private	Feb'y 6th, 1864	
Scruggs, John B	"	" 8tn, "	
Stephens, Henry M	"	Jau'y13th, "	
Stone, James A	"	" 1st, "	
Southard, Andrew J	"	Feb'y 4th, "	
Taylor, Robert A	"	" 18th, "	
Tony, Wm	"	Mar. 15th, "	Captured in Independence County, Ark., March 20, 1864.
Twilley, D. L	"	Jan'y 1st, "	
Watson, Benj. L	"	" 14th, "	
Watson, James A	"	" 11th, "	
Watson, Samuel W	"	" 16th, "	
Wilson, G. M. D	"	" 1st, "	
Wilson, J. R. P	"	" 1st, "	
Wackerly, Henry H	"	" 1st, "	Wounded in skirmish February 19, 1864.
Williams, Granville	"	" 1st, "	
Yates, Watsel A	"	" 1st, "	
Died.			
Mathis, Jesse C	Private	Jan'y 30th,1864	Died at Batesville, Ark., March 7th, 1864.
Evens, Thos. J	"	" 1st, "	Died at Batesville, Ark., May 2d, 1864.

STATE OF ARKANSAS,
A. G. O., Little Rock, September 27, 1871.

I certify that this roll exhibits a true copy from records on file in this office of Co. A, 4th Ark. Mounted Infantry.

KEYES DANFORTH,
Adjutant-General.

Examined and approved August 22, 1871.

ELISHA BAXTER,
Late Provisional Colonel of the 4th Arkansas Mounted Infantry Volunteers.

(Indorsed:) Muster-roll of Company A, of the 4th Regiment of Arkansas Mounted Infantry Volunteers, from the —— day of ——, 186-, to the —— day of ——, 186-.

STATE OF ARKANSAS,
County of Independence, ss:

On this 22d day of August, A. D. 1871, personally appeared before me, a county clerk in and for the county and State aforesaid, Taylor A. Baxter, of Independence County, and State of Arkansas, who, being duly sworn according to law, declares and says that he is the identical person named in the foregoing muster-roll of Company A, of the Fourth Regiment of Arkansas Mounted Infantry Volunteers, as captain; that he served as such captain during the time therein indicated; that the above is a true copy of a muster-roll made by me at the time said company was discharged, on the 3d day of June, 1864, and at that time filed in the office of the adjutant-general of Arkansas, and reflects the condition of said company at that time; that this company was raised principally in the county of Independence, State of Arkansas; that the company was, at different times, while in the service, stationed at Batesville, Jacksonport, and De Vall's Bluff, Ark., and was discharged while at the latter place; that the company performed full and active military duty from the date of enlistment to the day of discharge; that while in service a number of the men used their own private horses, while others were mounted by the government, and that no account of this was ever kept by this affiant.

TAYLOR A. BAXTER.

Subscribed and sworn to before me this 22d day of August, A. D. 1871.
[SEAL.] REUBEN HAYSHAM, *Clerk.*

II.—*Muster-in roll of Captain L. M. Harris's company, in the Fourth Regiment (——— Brigade) of Arkansas Inf. Volunteers, commanded by Colonel Elisha Baxter, called into the service of the United States by order from Maj. Gen'l F. Steele, com'd'g Dep't Ark's, from the ——— day of ———, 186- (date of this muster), for the term of one year, unless sooner discharged.*

Number of each grade.	Names, present and absent.	Rank.	Age.	When.	Where.	By whom enrolled.	Period.	Remarks.
1	L. M. Harris	Captain		1864. Jan'y 1	Batesville	L. M. Harris	One year	
1	Brice M. Garner	1st sergt	40	1	"	"	"	
2	William Ash	2d "	24	1	"	"	"	
3	David C. Bradford	3d "	30	1	"	"	"	
4	Henry Peters	4th "	22	1	"	"	"	
1	Allen, George W	Private	38	Mch. 15	"	"	"	
2	Allen, Thos. E	"	37	"	"	"	"	
3	Brown, Wm. H	"	21	Jan'y 1	"	"	"	
4	Brantley, Benj. F	"	44	Mch. 15	"	"	"	
5	Brazeal, William	"	37	20	"	"	"	
6	Boehm, Andrew	"	40	Jan'y 1	"	"	"	
7	Boehm, William	"	18	"	"	"	"	
8	Bishop, William	"	24	"	"	"	"	
9	Brown, George	"	26	"	"	"	"	
10	Cornwall, John R	"	41	Mch. 15	"	"	"	
11	Chambers, Wm. R	"	24	Jan'y 1	"	"	"	
12	Cartwright, John	"	30	Mch. 15	"	"	"	
13	Compton, Thos. J	"	26	Jan'y 1	"	"	"	
14	Ducker, John L	"	40	Mch. 1	"	"	"	
15	Daniels, William	"	29	"	"	"	"	
16	Eoff, Stephen	"	21	Jan'y 1	"	"	"	
17	Emmons, Griffin	"	19	20	"	"	"	
18	Emmons, Jno. W	"	17	Feb'y 15	"	"	"	
19	Elliott, Stephen	"	24	15	"	"	"	
20	Ellis, Wm	"	29	"	"	"	"	
21	Gadbury, Wm. H	"	23	Jan'y 1	"	"	"	
22	Gibson, Lebanon J	"	24	Mch. 1	"	"	"	
23	Gibson, Wm. S	"	21	"	"	"	"	
24	Harp, Wm. H	"	20	Feb'y 15	"	"	"	
25	Harp, Jno. L	"	24	15	"	"	"	
26	Hendricks, Jas. K. P	"	18	15	"	"	"	
27	Hendricks, Isaac B	"	33	15	"	"	"	
28	Hufstadler, Jacob	"	27	15	"	"	"	

Died in hospital, Batesville, Ark., M'ch 26th, 1864.

No.	Name	Age	Date
29	Hubbell, L. B	35	Jan'y 1
30	Huntley, Charles	24	" 1
31	Hull, George	24	" 1
32	Hakson, Geo. W	25	Mch. 1
33	Hammonds, Jas. H	25	Jan'y 1
34	Hooten, Elijah	26	
35	Halsenback, David C	24	Mch. 15
36	Hilton, Jessee W	18	" 15
37	Hilton, Jas. T	25	" 20
38	Ivey, James	18	" 20
39	Ivey, Greene	30	" 1
40	Lindsey, Jas. H	18	" 15
41	Lancaster, Allen P	23	Jan'y 1
42	Lancaster, James M	27	" 1
43	Lancaster, Perrin W	27	Mch. 15
44	Lancaster, Charles	23	" 15
45	Lindsey, Dixon M	19	Jan'y 1
46	Laveaua, Archie	20	Feb'y15
47	Lemmons, Amos J	20	Jan'y 1
48	Lemmons, Jno. T	24	
49	Michael, George W	34	" 15
50	Milligan, James	18	
51	McCorkle, Thomas	29	
52	McCorkle, Samuel	23	Feb'y15
53	Melton, Thomas	22	" 23
54	Noblin, Saul J	27	Mch. 20
55	Noblin, Cullen	36	" 20
56	Nichols, Edmund	30	Feb'y15
57	Nichols, Joseph	31	Jan'y 1
58	Puryear, James M	24	" 1
59	Pollard, James H	30	
60	Pruitt, Lewis H	44	
61	Parker, Milton J	26	
62	Peters, John	36	Mch.
63	Payne, Anderson H	27	Jan'y 1
64	Prichard, Henry J	27	Feb'y15
65	Prichard, James H	25	Jan'y 1
66	Philbrook, Samuel	38	" 29
67	Pyland, John E	21	
68	Reid, Henry	29	Mch.
69	Rowe, James	29	" 15
70	Russell, Wm. M	37	
71	Stafford, Wm. H	18	Jan'y 1
72	Sanders, W. F	43	
73	Stamps, John	30	
74	Stark, Frank	25	Feb'y15
75	Suoblin, Thomas	29	" 15
76	Slayton, Green D	30	" 15
77	Slayton, Wm. T	28	Apr. 1
78	Simms, Wm S	18	Mch. 15
79	Treadway, Wm. H	25	

H.—*Muster-in roll of Captain L. M. Harris' company, in the Fourth Regiment (——— Brigade) of Arkansas Inf. Volunteers, &c.*—Continued.

Number of each grade.	Names, present and absent.	Rank.	Age.	When.	Where.	By whom enrolled.	Period.	Remarks.
				1864.				
80	Teal, Andrew J	Private	31	Feb'y 15	Batesville	L. M. Harris	One year	
81	Terrill, Wm. C	"	30		"	"		
82	Vaughn, Jno. M	"	18		"	"		
83	Warlick, James W	"	31	Mch. 15	"	"		
84	Wilson, Edward C	"	22	Jan'y 1	"	"		
85	Williams, Amasa M	"	18	"	"	"		
86	Williams, Asa	"	19	"	"	"		
87	Williams, Anderson A	"	22	"	"	"		
88	White, John	"	29					
89	Waller, George	"	24					Killed in skirmish at Lunenberg, Ark., Jan'y 22, 1864

I.—*Muster-roll of Captain Moses Ford, Company (—,) of the 4th Regiment of Mounted Inf. Vol's (Ark.), United States Army, Colonel Elisha Baxter, from the 1st day of January, 1864, when last mustered, to the 2d day of June, 1864.*

No.	Names, present and absent.	Rank.	Joined for service and enrolled at general rendezvous. Commencement of first payment by time.				Remarks.
			When.	Where.	By whom.	Period.	
1	Moses Ford	Captain	1864. Jan. 1	Batesville, Ark		One year	
1	Robert S. Saunders	1st sergt	Ap'l 15	Batesville	Moses Ford	One year	
2	Chas. W. White	Sergt	15	"	"	"	
3	Carey Mosier	do	Jan'y 1	"	"	"	
4	Robert J. Baker	do	" 15	"	"	"	
1	Wm. J. Daniels	Corp	15	"	"	"	Killed in action Feb. 15.
2	Henry A. Miller	"	1	"	"	"	
3	Martin Speaks, sr	"	Ap'l 15	"	"	"	
4	Wm. M. Younger	"	Jan'y 1	"	"	"	
5	Wm. M. Ray	"	1	"	"	"	
6	Marcus P. Sipe	"	Feb. 1	"	"	"	
1	Adrian, George W.	Private	Ap'l 20	Batesville	Moses Ford		
2	Adkinson, William	"	May 1	"	"	"	
3	Bundy, William H	"	Mc'h 15	"	"	"	
4	Blue, William J	"	Jan'y 1	"	"	"	
5	Blue, Joseph	"	1	"	"	"	
6	Boyar, John H	"	15	"	"	"	
7	Baugs, Jacob	"		"	"	"	
8	Blagg, Samuel	"	Ap'l 1	"	"	"	
9	Blake, Samuel T	"	Jan'y 1	"	"	"	
10	Brown, Neal S.	"	15	"	"	"	
11	Bramlet, John T	"	15	"	"	"	
12	Barksdale, John T	"	Ap'l 1	"	"	"	
13	Brooks, James W	"		"	"	"	
14	Buckhart, John H	"	15	"	"	"	
15	Bundy, Ransom C	"	May 1	"	"	"	
16	Beekham, Rody	"	1	"	"	"	
17	Beekham, John	"	1	"	"	"	
18	Cunningham, Wm. P	"	Feb. 1	"	"	"	Died in hospital at Batesville, March 19 1864.
19	Clark, Henry C	"	Jan'y 1	"	"	"	
20	Coggershall, James K	"		"	"	"	
21	Coggershall, William	"		"	"	"	
22	Call, Harrison	"	15	"	"	"	
23	Canard, Joseph	"	Mc'h 15	"	"	"	
24	Dodd, Wm. J. C.	"	Feb. 1	"	"	"	

I.—*Muster-roll of Captain Moses Ford, Company* (—), *of the 4th Regiment of Mounted Inf. Vol's* (Ark.), *&c.—Continued.*

No.	Names, present and absent	Rank	When	Where	By whom	Period	Remarks
			1864.				
25	Davis, James C. C	Private	Feb. 1	Batesville	Moses Ford	One year	
26	Davis, William	"	M'ch 15	"		"	
27	Dodd, Benjamin H	"	Ap'l 15	"		"	
28	Fishback, Henry	"	Jan'y 1	"		"	
29	Fishback, Charles	"	Jan'y 1	"		"	
30	Ferguson, George	"	M'ch 15	"		"	
31	Granger, Alexander	"	Jan'y 1	"		"	
32	Grisso, James W	"	" 15	"		"	
33	Goodwin, Benjamin	"		"		"	
34	Grimes, David H	"	Feb. 1	"		"	
35	Greenway, James T	"	Ap'l 15	"		"	
36	Harrison, Albert A	"	May 1	"		"	
37	Johnson, John L	"	Ap'l 15	"		"	
38	Johnson, Elisha B	"	Jan'y 15	"		"	
39	Johnson, William O	"	" 15	"		"	
40	Jones, James F	"	" 15	"		"	
41	Klinger, Charles	"	Ap'l 15	"		"	
42	Kellian, Joseph	"	Jan'y 1	"		"	
43	Locke, William I	"	" 15	"		"	
44	Lively, Carter	"	Ap'l 1	"		"	
45	Mosier, Burrill A	"		"		"	
46	Mills, James F	"	Jan'y 1	"		"	
47	Mosier, John J	"	" 1	"		"	
48	McLaughlin, Mark B	"	Feb. 1	"		"	
49	Martin, Napol-on	"		"		"	
50	Mosier, John R	"	M'ch 15	"		"	
51	Mosier, Jacob	"	" 15	"		"	
52	Martin, Daniel	"		"		"	
53	Pumphrey, Franklin	"	Ap'l 1	"		"	
54	Preston, Charles F	"	Jan'y 1	"		"	
55	Painter, John W	"	" 1	"		"	
56	Pearce, Rayford	"	" 28	"		"	
57	Pittman, Matthew L	"		"		"	
58	Pramparin, Victor	"	Ap'l 1	"		"	
59	Russell, Christopher C	"	Jan'y 15	"		"	
60	Ray, John F	"	Jan'y 1	"		"	
61	Roby, James	"	" 1	"		"	
62	Collins, Charles	"	" 1	"		"	
63	Beamer, David	"	Ap'l 15	"		"	

No.	Name	
64	Sipus, William S	Jany 1
65	Sipus, Jacob P	1
66	Sipus, Franklin	1
67	Sipus, Rufus	1
68	Smith, Enoch	1
69	Smith, Leonidas	1
70	Sanders, John F	1
71	Sommers, William	1
72	Sullivan, Joseph D	Feb 1
73	Smith, Leander	Mch 1
74	Scorgrins, Isaac	Apl 15
75	Scott, Samuel	
76	Speaks, Martin, jr	Jany 1
77	Whiting, John W	Apl 15
78	Whitfield, Reuben	
79	Wor, Esidore	15
80	Woodvill, George W	20
81	Young, Andrew J	Jany 1
82	Young, William T	1

(Indorsed:) Muster roll Capt. Moses Ford's, of Company ——, of the 4th Regiment of Ark's Mounted Infantry Volunteers, from the 1st day January, 1864, to the 2d day of June, 1864.

NOTE.—These men were enlisted and were immediately placed upon active duty, in which they continued until the date of their disbandment at Duvall's Bluff, Arks., June 2d, 1864, by orders from Dept. Headquarters, 7th corps, Little Rock, Arks. They were never regularly mustered or paid; only sworn in and placed on duty.

I certify, on honor, that this muster roll is made out in the manner required by the printed notes; that it exhibits the true state of Captain Moses Ford's Company ——, of the (4) Fourth Regiment of Ark. M'ted Inf. Vols. for the period herein mentioned; that the "Remarks" set opposite the name of each officer and soldier are accurate and just; and that the "Recapitulation" exhibits in every particular the true state of the company, as required by Regulations and the Rules and Articles of War.

Station: Duvall's Bluff, Ark.
Date: June 2d, 1864.
(Signed)

MOSES FORD,
Commanding the Company.

J.—*Muster-roll of Captain T. A. Baxter's company (A) of the 4th Mounted Infantry Regiment of Arkansas Vols., United States Army, Colonel E. Baxter, from the first day of January, 1864, when organized, to the second day of June, 1864, when disbanded by Special Orders No. 121, dated Headquarters Department of Arkansas, June 2nd, 1864.*

No.	Names, present and absent.	Rank.	When.	Where.	By whom.	Period.	Pay due for use of horse & equipments. From what time.	To what time.	Names, present June 2d, 1864, when disbanded.	Money value of clothing drawn. $ Cs.	Remarks.
1	T. A. Baxter	Captain	Jan. 1, '64	Batesville, Ark.	Col. Baxter	1 year			T. A. Baxter		Com'd'g reg't since March 25, '64.
1	John W. Ayres	1st lieut.	Jan. 1, '64	Batesville, Ark.	Col. Baxter	1 year			John W. Ayres		Com'd'g company since March 25, '64.
1	Noel G. Reaves	2d lieut.	Jan. 1, '64	Batesville, Ark.	Col. Baxter	1 year			Noel G. Reaves		
1	Thos. M. Tyer	1st sergt.	Jan. 1, '64	Batesville, Ark.	Col. Baxter	1 year	Jan. 1, '04	May 20, '64	Thos. M. Tyer	39 75	
2	John W. Carter	Sergt.	Jan. 1, '64	"	"	1	"	March 10, '64	John W. Carter	39 75	
3	W. J. Roach	"	Jan. 1, '64	"	"	1	"	March 15, '64	W. J. Roach	37 45	
4	C. J. Fuller	"	Jan. 1, '64	"	"	1	"		C. J. Fuller	38 20	
5	M. J. Bradley	"	Jan. 1, '64	"	"	1	"	Feb. 19, '64	M. J. Bradley	46 75	Wounded in skirmish with enemy Feb. 19, '64.
1	W. A. Curtis	Corporal	Jan. 1, '64	Batesville, Ark.	Col. Baxter	1 year	Jan. 1, '64	Apr. 23, '64	W. A. Curtis	33 26	
2	A. J. Sherrill	"	Jan. 17, '64	"	"	1			A. J. Sherrill	34 65	
3	W. H. Fuller	"	Dec. 15, '63	Jacksonport, Ark	"	1	Dec. 15, '63	Feb. 19, '64	W. H. Fuller	29 80	
4	J. C. Reynolds	"	Jan. 15, '64	Batesville, Ark.	"	1			J. C. Reynolds	32 00	
5	E. E. Rushing	"	Jan. 1, '64	"	"	1			E. E. Rushing	30 10	
6	J. D. Massey	"	"	"	"	1	Jan. 1, '64	Feb. 19, '64	J. D. Massey	38 30	
7	J. M. Freeman	"	Jan. 1, '64	"	"	1	"	March 20, '64	J. M. Freeman	39 80	
8	Jas. H. Wyatt	"	Jan. 1, '64	"	"	1			Jas. H. Wyatt	45 80	
1	Allen, Marcus	Private	April 6, '64	Batesville, Ark.	Col. Baxter	1 year			Marcus Allen	39 25	
2	Arnold, Ralph	"	Jan. 1, '64	"	"	1			Ralph Arnold	39 25	
3	Blevins, Alcana	"	March 15, '64	"	"	1			Alcana Blevins	35 26	
4	Berry, Spencer	"	Jan. 1, '64	"	"	1			Spencer Berry	38 16	
5	Bell, Wm. W.	"	"	"	"	1			Wm. W. Bell	42 28	
6	Bass, Wm. M.	"	Feb. 4, '64	"	"	1			Wm. M. Bass	38 25	
7	Blevins, Oliver C.	"	Feb. 5, '64	"	"	1			Oliver C. Blevins	40	
8	Bryant, Wm. H.	"	Jun. 29, '64	"	"	1			Wm. H. Bryant	38 25	
9	Brown, Grigsby	"	Jun. 1, '64	"	"	1	Jan. 1, '64	Feb. 19, '64	Grigsby Brown	37 26	Wounded in skirmish with enemy Feb. 19, '64.
10	Burgess, Leroy	"	1, '64	"	"	1			Leroy Burgess	39 15	
11	Chastain, Abner	"	April 6, '64	"	"	1			Abner Chastain	33 27	
12	Chastain, Joseph	"	April 6, '64	"	"	1			Joseph Chastain	39 14	

No.	Name			Sick in Independence Co., Ark., since April 20, '64.	Enlisted
13	Benj. F. Chastain	38	28		
14	Jno. M. Craven	36	40		March 17, '64
15	N. C. Chamness	39	46		Jan. 13, '64
16	W. P. Churchwell	40	18		
17	A. J. Coveston	36	14		March 8, '64
18	John Curtis	40	18		Jan. 1, '64
19	Wm. R. Custis	39	28		
20	Elijah Davis	41	27		May 8, '64
21	David F. Evans		22		
22	John T. Evans	24	16		May 2, '64
23	John O. Fox	40	75		Jan. 30, '64
24	Ellison Foust	38	17	Jan. 1, '64	
25	C. C. Forrester	29	18	April 23, '64	Jan. 23, '64
26	Robt. C. Forrester	40	20		March 26, '64
27	Wm. French	38	14		Jan. 23, '64
28	Ellis A. Furgison	37	26	Jan. 23, '64	Jan. 1, '64
29	John G. Holland	43	26		
30	Frank S. Harris	42	15	May 5, '64	Feb. 18, '64
31	Elijah Holt	40	10		Jan. 18, '64
32	Pleasant Holt	43	20	March 10, '64	Jan. 1, '64
33	F. M. Hughes	38	20	March 24, '64	Jan. 1, '64
34	W. J. Hunt	39	25		Jan. 1, '64
35	S. M. Hawk	38	20		Feb. 17, '64
36	John Knight	40	25		March 5, '64
37	J. J. Knight	32	20	Jan. 1, '64	Jan. 1, '64
38	M. V. Knight	42	13	April 12, '64	March 5, '64
39	L. T. Knight	39	15		Feb. 17, '64
40	L. F. Knight	40	16		April 8, '64
41	James Lacy	38	28		Jan. 6, '64
42	James Lacy	35	25		Feb. 12, '64
43	Wm. H. H. Liles	40	18		Jan. 4, '64
44	John R. Lemons	43	50		March 15, '64
45	Samuel Lemons	39	18		Jan. 25, '64
46	Holland Markham	36	27		Jan. 14, '64
47	Wm. J. Mathis	37	75		
48	Joshua C. Meritt	40		April 24, '64	Jan. 19, '64
49	John C. McAfee	41	77		
50	Wm. Marshall	40	70	April 2, '64	Jan. 1, '64
51	Richard D. Meeks	39	80		Jan. 20, '64
52	Wm. P. Nunn	39	12		
53	Wm. Nunnelly	42	75	March 1, '64	Feb. 1, '64
54	Thos. R. Owen	40	17		Jan. 1, '64
55	Jas. Overstreet	39	20		Jan. 30, '64
56	Wm. L. Ozment	40	17	Feb. 19, '64	
57	Robt. W. Pool	42	16		March 15, '64
58	Joseph Pickel	38	25		Jan. 1, '64
59	Geo. M. Reynolds	50	28		
60	Jackson Rhoades	41			Jan. 1, '64
61	Geo. D. Snodgrass	40	26		Feb. 6, '64
62	W. K. N. Scruggs	38	26		

J.—Muster-roll of Captain T. A. Baxter's company (A) of the 4th Mounted Infantry Regiment of Arkansas Vols., United States Army, &c.—Continued.

No.	Names, present and absent.	Rank.	Joined for service and enrolled at general rendezvous. Commencement of first payment by time.				Pay due for use of horse & equipments.		Names, present June 2d, 1864, when disbanded.	Money value of clothing drawn.	Remarks.
			When.	Where.	By whom.	Period	From what time.	To what time.			
63	Scruggs, John	Private	Feb. 8, '64	Batesville, Ark	Col. Baxter	1 year			John B. Scruggs	$37 17	
64	Stephens, Henry H.	"	Jan. 13, '64	"	"	1 "			Henry H. Stephens.	39 26	
65	Stone, Jas. A	"	" 1, '64	"	"	1 "			Jas. A. Stone.	40	
66	Southard, Andrew J	"	Feb. 4, '64	"	"	1 "			Andrew J. Southard.	41 27	
67	Taylor, Robt. A	"	" 18, '64	"	"	1 "	March 20, '64	April 10, '64	Robt. A. Taylor.	37	Captured by the enemy in Independence Co., Ark., March 20, '64.
68	Toney, Wm	"	March 15, '64	"	"	1 "				36 24	
69	Twilley, D. L.	"	Jan. 1, '64	"	"	1 "			D. L. Twilley.	39 15	
70	Watson, Benj. L	"	" 14, '64	"	"	1 "			Benj. Watson	40 14	
71	Watson, Jas. A	"	" 11, '64	"	"	1 "			Jas. A. Watson	36 14	
72	Watson, Sam'l W	"	" 16, '74	"	"	1 "	March 13, '64	April 18, '64	Sam'l W. Watson	39 15	
73	Wilson, G. M. D.	"	" 1, '64	"	"	1 "			G. M. D. Wilson	40 15	
74	Wilson, J. K. P	"	" 1, '64	"	"	1 "			J. K. P. Wilson	41	
75	Wackerly, Henry H.	"	" 1, '64	"	"	1 "	Jan. 1, '64	March 10, '64	Henry H. Wackerly.	33 15	Wounded in skirmish with enemy Feb. 19, '64.
76	Williams, Granville.	"	" 1, '64	"	"	1 "	1, '64	April 10, '64	Granville Williams.	41 12	
77	Yates, Watsell A	"	" 1, '64	"	"	1 "			Watsel A. Yates.	39 16	
78	Fuller, F. N.	"	" 1, '64	"	"	1 "	Jan. 1, '64	April 11, '64	F. N. Fuller.	40 17	
	DIED.										
1	Mathis, Jesse C	Private	Jan. 30, '64	Batesville, Ark	Col. Baxter	1 year				28 15	Died of disease at Batesville, Ark., March 7, '64.
2	Evans, Thos. J	"	" 1, '64	"	"	1 "	Jan. 1, '64	April 11, '64		39 14	Died of disease at Batesville, Ark., May 2, '64.

RECAPITULATION.

	Captain.	1st lieutenants.	2d lieutenants.	B'v't 2d lient.	Sergeants.	Corporals.	Buglers.	Musicians.	Farriers and black-smiths.	Artificers.	Privates.	Total commissioned.	Total enlisted.	Aggregate.
Present:														
For duty	1	1			5	6					68	2	79	81
On extra or daily duty						2					8		10	10
Sick														
In arrest or confinement														
Absent:														
On detached service			1									1		1
With leave														
Prisoners											1		1	1
Sick											1		1	1
In arrest or confinement														
Strength, present and absent	1	1	1		5	8					78	3	91	94

(Indorsed:) Muster-roll of Company A of the 4th regiment of Ark. Mounted Inf, from the 1st day of Jan'y, 1864, to the 2nd day of June, 1864.

NOTE.—This company was organized and reported for duty to Col. Livingston, 1st Nebraska Cav., com'd'g Dist. of Northeast Ark., at Batesville, Ark., on the 1st day of Jan., 1864, and from that time until disbanded did a proportional share of duty with the troops of the district.

I certify, on honor, that this muster-roll is made out in the manner required by the *printed notes*; that it exhibits the true state of Captain T. A. Baxter's company (A) of the 4th Mounted Infantry Regiment of Arkansas Vols. for the period herein mentioned; that [the "Remarks" set opposite the name of each officer and soldier are accurate and just; and that the "Recapitulation" exhibits in every particular the true state of the company, as required by Regulations and the Rules and Articles of War.

Station: Duvall's Bluff, Ark.
Date: June 2d, 1864.

JNO. W. AYRES,
1st Lt., Commanding the Company.

K.—*Master-roll of Lieut. Geo. W. Robertson's Company , of the Fourth Regiment of Mounted Infantry Volunteers, United States Army, Colonel Elisha Baxter, from the thirteenth day of January, 1864, when organized, to the third day of June, 1864, when disbanded by special order No. 121, Dept. of Ark.*

No.	Names, present and absent.	Rank.	When.	Where.	By whom.	Period.	Money value of clothing drawn during enlistment.	Last paid. From—	Last paid. To—	Names present.	Remarks.
1	Geo. W. Robertson	1st lieut						Furnished horse and horse equipments.			Enlisted 1st lieutenant Jan'y 28th, 1864
1	Solomon K. Chandler	1st serg't	Dec 1st,1863	Jacksonport, Ark.	Lt. Geo. W. Robertson.	One year	37 48	Dec. 1st, 1863	May 23d, '64	Solomon K. Chandler.	1st serg't from Jan'y 30th, 1864, to June 3d, 1864.
1	J. H. Jones	Serg't	1st, '63	"	"	"	39 82	" 1st, 1863	" 23, '64	J. H. Jones	Serg't from Jan'y 30th, 1864, to June 3d, 1864.
1	G. H. Pinkston	Corp'l	1st, '63	"	"	"	37 02	Jan. 27th, '64	Ap'l 10, "	G. H. Pinkston	Corporal from Jan'y 30th, 1864, to June 3d, '64.
2	G. W. Good	"	Jany. 27,'64	Batesville.	"	"	30 19			G. W. Good	Corporal from Feb'y 10th, '64, to June 3d, '64.
3	J. E. Gifford	"	" 30, "	"	"	"	35 58			J. E. Gifford	Corporal from Feb'y 10, '64, to June 3d, '64.
1	Adams, B. F.	Private	Dec. 1st,'63	Jacksonport, Ark	Lt. Robertson	One year	37 34	Dec. 1st, 1863	Feb. 1st, '64	B. F. Adams	
2	Anderson, Isaac	"	Jany. 18,'64	Batesville,	"	"	35 54			Isaac Anderson.	
3	Anderson, J. W.	"	Dec. 15,'63	Jacksonport,	"	"	56 25	Dec. 15th, '63	Feb. 10, '64	J. W. Anderson.	Lost horse and horse equipments in a skirmish at Holt's Mill, Feb. 10th, '64, also was captured and had clothing taken from him by the enemy.
4	Bishop, Joseph	Private	Jany. 16,'64	Batesville, Ark	Lt. Robertson	One year	44 74	Jany 18th, '64	May 30th, '64	Joseph Bishop	
5	Bishop, W. A.	"	" 22, "	"	"	"	34 40			W. A. Bishop	
6	Bryson, R. J.	"	Dec. 1, '63	Jacksonport,	"	"	37 02	Dec. 1st, '63	Feb. 10, '64	R. J. Bryson	
7	Barber, A. A.	"	Mch. 22,'64	Batesville,	"	"	27 00			A. A. Barber	
8	Chandler, B. F.	Private	Dec. 1, '63	Jacksonport, Ark	Lt. Robertson	One year	37 47	Dec. 1st, '63	May 23d, '64	B. F. Chandler	
9	Cochran, Henry	"	" 15, "	Batesville,	"	"	35 66			Henry Cochran	
10	Caster, J. E.	"	Jany. 27,'64	Batesville,	"	"	31 33			J. E. Carter	
11	Dugger, A. M.	Private	Dec. 1st,'63	Jacksonport, Ark	Lt. Robertson	One year	34 57			A. M. Dugger	

No.	Name	Rank	Date of enlistment	Place of enlistment	By whom enlisted	Period	Amount	Name	Date	Remarks
12	Doin, Wm	Private	Mch. 29, '64	Batesville,		One year	17 00	Wm. Doin		Deserted May 30th, 1864, at Jacksonport, Arkansas.
13	Embry, G. M	"	Mch. 23, '64	Batesville, Ark	Lt. Robertson	"	28 00	G. M. Embry		
14	Embry, W. M	"	"	"	"	"	28 00	W. M. Embry		
15	Embry, D. C	"	"	"	"	"	24 10	D. C. Embry		
16	Ford, B. F	Private	Jany. 27, '64	Batesville, Ark	Lt. Robertson	One year	33 13	B. F. Ford		
17	Ford, W. R	"	27, '64	"	"	"	30 38	W. R. Ford		
18	Good, J. J	Private	Jany. 15, '64	Batesville, Ark	Lt. Robertson	One year	27 58	J. J. Good	Dec. 1st, '03	
19	Gire, W. H	"	Dec. 1, '63	Jacksonport, Ark	"	"	40 32		Feb. 15th, '64	
20	Hicks, G. C	Private	Mch. 17, '64	Batesville, Ark	Lt. Robertson	One year	29 05	G. C. Hicks		
21	Hamby, A. R. D	"	Feb. 1st, "	"	"	"	33 38	A. R. D. Hamby		
22	Hamby, A. N. M	"	1st, "	Jacksonport, "	"	"	30 31	A. N. M Hamby		
23	Huff, W. B	"	Dec. 15, '63	Batesville, "	"	"	34 19	W. B. Huff		
24	Hall, E. E	"	Jany. 25, '64	"	"	"	35 64	E. E. Hall		
25	Hall, I. A	"	27, '64	"	"	"	34 83	I. A. Hall		
26	Harris, Simeon	"	14, '64	"	"	"	30 40	Simeon Harris	Jan'y 27, '64 May 30, 64	
27	Hoent, A. M	"	Mch. 14, '64	"	"	"	26 49	A. M. Hoent		
28	Hawkins, S. D	"	21, '64	"	"	"	27 89	S. D. Hawkins		
29	Johnson, R. D	Private	Mch. 22, '64	Batesville, Ark	Lt. Robertson	One year	19 02	R. D. Johnson	Jan'y25th,'64 May 30, 64	Captured and his clothing taken from him by the enemy.
30	Lane, Bird	"	Jany. 25, "	"	"	"	33 54	Bird Lane		
31	Lingo, Mose	Mch.	9, "	Jacksonport, Ark	"	"	23 18	Mose Lingo		
32	Medee, J. K. P	Private	Dec. 15, '63	"	Lt. Robertson	One year	33 03	J. K. P. Mdiee.	Dec. 15, '63 M'ch 1st, '64	
33	McCrory, F. E	"	1st, '63	Batesville,	"	"	38 59	F. E. McCrory	Dec. 1st, '63 Feb. 1st, '64	
34	McLead Neill		Feb. 1st, '64				59 45	Neil McLead		
35	Morgan, J. D		Jany. 15, '64				15 51	J. D. Morgan		
36	Massey, Eli		14, '64				37 04	Eli Massey		
37	Mobley, Calvin		Feb. 18, '64				30 30	Calvin Mobley		
38	Montgomory, James		Apl. 12, "				11 84	James Montgom-ery		
39	Norris, W. R	Private	Jany. 25, '64	Batesville, Ark	Lt. Roberts n	One year	52 80	W. R. Norris	Jan'y28th,'64 Feb. 25th,'64	Captured and his clothing taken from him by the enemy.
40	Pinkston, Phineas	Private	Dec. 15, '63	Jacksonport, Ark	Lt. Robertson	One year	37 77	Phineas Pinkston	Dec. 15th, '64	Deserted May 30th, 1864, at Jacksonport, Arkansas.
41	Prevett, Jesse	"	Jany. 18, '64	Batesville,	"	"	33 02	Jesse Trevett	March 1st, '64	
42	Price, J. G	"	Mch. 14, "	"	"	"	19 61	J. G. Price		
43	Price, L. C	"	14, "	"	"	"	29 17	L. C. Price		
44	Price, William	"	Apl. 1st, "	"	"	"	14 09			
45	Rodgers, G. M. D	Private	Dec. 1st, '63	Jacksonport, Ark	Lt. Robertson	One year	37 02	G. M. D. Rodgers	March 1, '64	Lost horse and equipments in action Feb. 10th, 1864.
46	Rinsick, Henry	"	Jany. 28, '61	Batesville,	"	"	51 27	Henry Rinsick	Feb. 10, 64	
47	Suddrith, Gerard	Private	Dec. 15, '63	Jacksonport, Ark	Lt. Robertson	One year	35 44	Gerard Suddith	Dec.15th, '63 Feb. 15, '64	
48	Swick, G. W	"	Jany. 27, '64	Batesville,	"	"	31 33	G. W. Swick		
49	Swope, John	"	Dec. 15, '63	Jacksonport,	"	"	37 04	John Swope		
50	Scoggins, G. W	"	Mch. 14, '64	Batesville,	"	"	26 62	G. W. Scoggins		

K.—*Master-roll of Lieut. Geo. W. Robertson's Company , of the Fourth Regiment of Mounted Infantry Volunteers, United States Army, &c.—Cont'd.*

| No. | Names, present and absent. | Rank. | Joined for service and enrolled at general rendezvous. Commencement of first payment by time. | | | | Money value of clothing drawn during enlistment. | Last paid. | | Names present. | Remarks. |
			When.	Where.	By whom.	Period.		From—	To—		
							$ Cts.				
51	Simpson, A. A.	Private	Jany. 29,'64	Batesville, Ark	Lt. Robertson	One year	25 54			A. A. Simpson	
52	Sellers, T. W.	"	" 20,"	"	"	"	34 72			T. W. Sellers	
53	Smith, J. E.	"	Feb. 5,"	"	"	"	32 01	Feb. 5th,'64	Ap'l 1st,'64	J. B. Smith	
54	Smith, W. T.	"	" 18,"	"	"	"	35 22			W. T. Smith	
55	Stout, H. H.	"	Mch. 22,"	"	"	"	27 00				Deserted May 30th, 1864, at Jacksonport, Ark.
56	Stevens, G. W.	Private	Apl. 26,'64	Batesville, Ark	Lt. G.W. Robertson	One year	18 04			G. W. Stevens	
57	Tindle, R. P.	"	Jany. 18,'64	"	"	"	31 99			R. P. Tindle	
58	Wolfe, John	Private	Jany. 25,'64	Batesville, Ark	Lt. G.W. Robertson	One year	31 58			John Wolfe	
59	Wilson, E. D.	"	Dec. 15,'63	"	"	"	44 54			E. D. Wilson	
60	Wasson, J. B.	"	Feb. 5,'64	"	"	"	32 78			J. B. Wasson	
61	Wilkinson, F. J.	"	" 5,"	"	"	"	31 30			F. J. Wilkinson	
62	Whillow, S. C.	"	Jan. 27,'64	"	"	"	29 35			S. C. Whillow	
63	Ward, Jasper	"	Apr. 18,'64	"	"	"	14 36				Deserted May 30th, 1864, at Jacksonport, Ark.
64	Wolfe, Daniel	"	Jany. 25,'64	"	"		30 51			David Wolfe	

RECAPITULATION.

	Captain	1st lieutenants	2d lieutenants	B'v't 2d lieut.	Sergeants	Corporals	Buglers	Musicians	Farriers and blacksmiths	Artificers	Privates	Total commissioned	Total enlisted	Aggregate
Present:														
For duty		1			2	3					60	1	65	66
On extra or daily duty														
Sick														
In arrest or confinement														
Absent:														
On detached service														
With leave														
Without leave														
Sick														
In arrest or confinement														
Strength, present and absent		1			2	3					60	1	65	66
ALTERATIONS SINCE LAST MUSTER.														
Joined:														
Recruits from depots														
Enlisted in company														
By re-enlistment														
By transfer or appointment														
From desertion														
Resigned.														
Discharged:														
Expiration of service														
For disability														
By sent. of G. C. martial														
By civil authority														
By order														
Transferred														
Died:														
Killed in action														
Of wounds														
From disease, &c														
Deserted.												4	4	4

(Indorsed:) Muster roll of Company B, of the Fourth Regiment of Ark. Mounted Inf't'y, from the 30th day of January, 1864, to the 3d day of June, 1864.

NOTE.—This Co. was organized Jan'y 30th, 1864, with 42 men, by electing Geo. W. Robertson 1st lieutenant; these recruits were in active service with the 3d Mo. and 1st Nebraska Cavalry, from date of enlistment until disbanded by Special Order 121, Dep't of Ark.

I certify, on honor, that this Muster Roll is made out in the manner required by the *printed notes;* that it exhibits the true state of Lieut. Geo. W. Robertson's Company (——), of the 4th Ark. M. I. V., Regiment of ——, for the period herein mentioned; that the "Remarks" set opposite the name of each officer and soldier are accurate and just; and that the "Recapitulation" exhibits in every particular the true state of the company, as required by Regulations and the Rules and Articles of War.

Station: Duvall's Bluff, Ark.
Date: June 3d, '64.

GEO. W. ROBERTSON,
1st Lt., Commanding the Company.

L.—*Muster-roll of field and staff of the 4th Regiment of Ark. M'td Inf'ry Volunteers, serving at Batesville, Ark., under the command of Col. L. R. Livingston, of the First Regiment of Nebraska Cav'ly Vol's, from the 15th day of November, 1863, when last mustered, to the second day of June, 1864.*

Names (including commissioned officers) present and absent.	Rank.	Enlisted.				Remarks.
		When.	Where.	By whom.	Period.	
		1863.				The field & staff (as well as the battalion) were on duty from November 15th, 1863 (date of entry into service), until June 2d, the date of discharge thro' orders received from h'dq'rs, Dep't of Ark. They were never regularly mustered nor paid. The only commission issued to any of the command was the order from Maj. Gen. Steele, com'd'g Dep't Ark., authorizing Col. Elisha Baxter to organize the battalion.
Elisha Baxter	Colonel	Nov. 15	Little Rock, Ark	Maj. Gen. Steele	One year	
Martin Beene	Adjutant	Nov. 15	Little Rock, Ark	Elisha Baxter	One year	
John J. Palmer	Q'rmaster	Nov. 15	Little Rock, Ark	Elisha Baxter	One year	

I certify, on honor, that this muster-roll is made out in the manner required by the printed notes; that it exhibits the true state of field and staff of the 4th Regiment of Arkansas Mounted Infantry Vol's for the period herein mentioned; that the "Remarks" set opposite the name of each officer and soldier are accurate and just; and that the "Recapitulation" exhibits in every particular the true state of the detachment, as required by Regulations and the Rules and Articles of War; and that all the officers and enlisted men belong to the same regiment.

Station, Duvall's Bluff, Ark.

Date, June 2d, 1864.

Commanding the Detachment.

O

www.ingramcontent.com/pod-product-compliance
Lightning Source LLC
Chambersburg PA
CBHW021636270326
41931CB00008B/1050